Life: 101
By
Paul D. Failla

Edited by: Nancy G. DiMonte

Life:101
Copyright 2013 by Paul D. Failla and Nancy G. DiMonte

Cover design and photograph by Nancy G. DiMonte

ISBN-13:978-1482786903
Failla, Paul D.
Edited by DiMonte, Nancy G.
Copyright 2013

Love, Peace

&

Happiness

"Learn to surround yourself with positive influences and realize your goals even when others may deflate you...... When told that what you are trying to attain is too difficult, let those words be the fuel that blasts you like a rocket into the stratosphere. "

~~~

Dedication

To those who have taught me how to embrace others, I write these words for you. I dedicate this book to the family and friends who have given their time to teach me life's lessons while showing me the path to a successful career and fulfilling existence. This book is a testament to the many people who have touched my heart and soul and remain as an inspiration to me. I thank you all for allowing me to play a role in your lives, and I am grateful for the lessons I have obtained from all of you. Finally, to my wife and daughters and the members of my immediate and extended family, I hope to give back as much as you have given me. Special thanks to my editor and friend, Nancy DiMonte, for her unselfish dedication, professionalism, knowledge, and insurmountable patience during this endeavor. "Paul"

I dedicate my part in this project to so many people who have been instrumental in my life as a wife, mother to a daughter and son, daughter, aunt, niece, sister, and friend. To my late husband, Tom, who never questioned the project but awaited its arrival. It has finally arrived and will be delivered to you with love and thanks for the support you have given me throughout our short lifespan together. However short, it was meaningful, much like the messages in this book—those of hope, caring, and courage. To Paul, I thank you for the time that we have spent on this project and for all that our families have shared during the conception of this book and for all the hearty laughs and tears. "Nancy"

" A wise young man said to his mother that he would never do anything crazy since he was raised by his mom and dad." He was fully assured that they raised him sensibly and that he would be sensible.

Preface

A quote will appear before each chapter in the hopes that it will inspire you to read further. All content brings forth a valuable message about life choices. Although written in somewhat of an abstract form (to inspire curiosity), the reader will extract what affects him or her and draw conclusions regarding the most appropriate actions to take when faced with compromising situations. Specific references will be alluded to with respect to the various topics. I hope you find yourself embedded in the messages and use them to prepare for an enlightened life course. Finally, I encourage the reader to take the journey with an open mind, a vision, an appreciation of humor, a heightened sense of self and a sense of solitude. Throughout each chapter I portray the advantages and disadvantages of life's decisions based on the best and worst case scenarios.

At the midpoint of the writing of this book I wrote,

*produced, and perform a one-man show titled, "**The Class of Life."** This theatrical experience, directed by Michael Moriarty, is a play that takes the audience on a journey which highlights my life, much like the stories in this book which highlight my career. The play begins on the last day of my career as a police officer. This day gives way to reminiscing about my motivation to become a police officer, my proud Italian heritage, my upbringing, and married life. Utilizing a blend of humor, drama, song, dance, and life experience, I take my audience on an emotional roller coaster through stories relating to all. This poignant presentation will surely touch the lives of those who value family, tradition, and comedy.*

It is my hope that you read the book and see the play.

Life:101

Table of Contents

Chapter 1 Introduction

When It Began

Life as a Cop

"They pay you for eight hours a day, you give them eight hours a day. Give one hundred percent, one hundred percent of the time. This is a work ethic to abide by."

For the first five years of my education, I was the only student at Paul and Rose University, so I received hands-on education from the founders of the school. After five years, they moved the university from Queens, New York further east on Long Island, and I moved with them for two reasons. First, I liked the school and secondly, I was on the "extended plan." No sooner did we move when a female student came to the campus. We accepted this student because she was my sister, Gioia, who today is a talented cosmetologist. In case you haven't figured it out, Paul, an eleven-year WWII navy veteran, with a reserved manner and keen sense of humor, and Rose, a talented custom

3

dressmaker with hands of gold and a truly outgoing personality, were my parents. My sister and I received an education from our parents that you can't buy at any college, university or learning institution. Little did we know that the lessons taught would impact us throughout our lives. Paul and Rose were the children of parents of Italian descent who immigrated to America to afford their children a good life in the "land of opportunity." Paul and Rose, who were born in America, took the old world values they received from their parents and passed them along to their children. I now find myself passing these same traditions to my children who hopefully will pass them along to my grandchildren someday. Traditional values such as character, honor, dignity, and respect were instilled and reinforced consistently. In addition, a strong work ethic was implanted through modeling by Paul and Rose. Paul often told me, "They pay you for eight hours a day; you give them eight hours a day." I've lived by this ethic, always giving one hundred percent one hundred percent of the time in all of my endeavors.

Life lessons included instilling and reinforcing the importance of values such as family, health, freedom, peace of mind, friendship, love, religious faith, and sense of humor. I consider these values my royal flush in spades. Although there are eight cards, it is not a misdeal. The eighth card (sense of humor) is a trump card because without a sense of humor you flounder in the real world. At Paul and Rose University you were not handed a list of words and asked to find the definitions in the dictionary; you lived everyday practicing and cherishing the aforementioned values. Respect of others, especially your elders, was protocol. Elders included parents, friends and elder relatives, who were referred to as "Mr., Mrs., Miss, Aunt or Uncle." A firm handshake with eye contact, a show of affection in the form of a hug and kiss for those you love was commonplace. Words including "Yes, No, Ma'am, Sir, Please, Thank You, You're Welcome, May I, and Excuse Me" were ingrained through rote which then became standard patterns of speech. Behavior patterns also developed through rote which included responsibility for completing schoolwork, chores, personal hygiene, along with allegiance to self, others, and country. At Paul and Rose University you were held accountable for everything you did that was right and everything you did that was wrong. When you were right, you were rewarded and when you were wrong, there were consequences. You paid the consequences because Paul and Rose knew any other way was stifling their children's growth into adulthood. Encouragement to undertake what appeared to be insurmountable odds was always provided. If at first you were unsuccessful, you were taught to use the experience as a learning tool and not accept failure as an alternative. Our parents lived to provide for their children so we could have a better life than they. I grew up surrounded by master storytellers. My parents' generation grew up listening to radio for their entertainment. Radio broadcasters back in their day could create vivid images with words as well as any television show does today. As a boy, I listened intently to the stories, their words, and paid close attention to their style of speaking. Hence, in today's world where everyone is accustomed to "bells and whistles," I engage my audiences mostly with words.

My father, one of eight children, with a limited formal education, wrote the "book on life" and possessed an immeasurable amount of common sense. My father started working at ten years of age to help his parents who were newcomers to this country. He would walk me through his former neighborhood in Queens, New York pointing out highlights of his childhood. As a young man my father, who lived through the Great Depression, would take jobs to make money to contribute to his family. No job was beneath him. He and his brothers would whitewash curbs and trees as it dressed up the neighborhood because the residents liked the way it looked and also so drivers could easily see the curbs and trees at night. He would walk with me and point out the former locations of the coal yard and ice factory where he worked. He explained that working as a delivery boy was important since the coal was needed to heat homes and the ice was used to keep food cold in the ice box, or refrigerator as we know it today. Those of my father's generation were humble enough to accept any and all work as an opportunity. My dad was paid about ten cents a week for his efforts, of which he gave eight cents to his dad. He would save two cents for himself and when he had a dime, he went to a movie theater where for that ten cents you could see two movies and buy candy. Unfortunately, when he started working at ten years old, he started smoking cigarettes. His generation did not know what we know today about the dangers of smoking. They used to advertise back in his day that smoking cigarettes was good for you. Before there were warnings on packs of cigarettes, my father used to tell me, "Son, if I thought this was good for you I would buy you a carton a day and sit with you until you smoked every cigarette in that carton." I recall him pointing to his chest, while holding a cigarette and saying, "Son I think this smoking is killing me" and sure enough, it did. My father passed from a smoking-related disease. Smoking killed my best friend in life. When my wife and I married, there were eighteen people in our wedding party including seven bridesmaids, seven ushers, a flower girl, a ring bearer, my wife's sister as a Maid of Honor, and my dad was my Best Man. Even though he is gone all these years he will forever live in my life, the life of my children, and hopefully all future generations of my family through the values he and my mother instilled in me which I have instilled in my children through their timeless lifelong lessons. On June 30, 1990, Paul left the living years leaving Rose to carry on tradition. Even though he is gone twenty-three years at the time of this writing, his words and lessons will stay with me forever as I pass them down to my children and others. My wife Dale has given me two of the greatest gifts one person can give another, namely my daughters, Gioia and Maria. Through the teachings by which Dale and I have been raised on, we have successfully passed down our value systems to our children who will one day hopefully continue to uphold these values and family traditions. We believe in a strong work ethic and have benefitted from this. Our daughters have attained many of their goals, as our oldest daughter has been in a career for several years related to her chosen field of business, and our youngest daughter is soon to graduate college and embark on a career in marketing. Dale has been most supportive in their efforts, and she and I continue to encourage the girls to reach for their highest aspirations. As of this writing we have been blessed with the news of our first daughter's growing family as she and her husband, Jay, welcome a baby in October. We are confident that she and her husband will combine all of the family values that surround them to raise their child.

I can't remember a time in my life when I didn't want to be a cop. I can't recall the exact moment, but perhaps the initial spark came when I lived in Queens where my friend's dad was a New York City police officer and role model; or perhaps as a young boy witnessing a police officer at a horrific motor vehicle accident; or perhaps respected relatives of mine who were police officers influenced my aspirations. I went through all my school years telling my teachers that I was going to be a cop. It was obvious that some took me seriously while others did not. The deal was sealed when I went to see the movie, "Serpico." I perceived him as a man of conviction who almost paid the ultimate price; his life, for his beliefs. He never wavered from his moral and ethical codes. Surely I was hooked. I researched police departments for possible employment throughout the country, from New York to California to Texas and Florida. The city of Tampa, Florida tested me and eventually I was hired as a police officer. Meantime, I was on the police list in Suffolk County, Long Island and when my grade was processed, I became a police officer in the county. After twenty-eight years, including service in Tampa, I concluded my career as an officer. I had a varied career which included patrol, a position as a recruit training instructor, police recruiter, and warrant enforcement officer. I always considered police work to be the "ultimate people" business. I judged my performance by my ability to effectively deal with people. Interpersonal skills combined with empathy, sympathy, compassion, intuitiveness, and common sense are traits of a quintessential police officer. Having made hundreds of arrests, I pride myself in the fact that I had no complaints referenced to civil rights or brutality violations. In fact, I can count on less than one hand the amount of times I had to use force to take a person into custody, and I can count on more than two hands the amount of times a person in custody thanked me after an arrest. I took from them everything that America stands for, namely freedom, and yet they thanked me because I treated them as I would like to be treated in a similar situation.

Attaining goals is very important, especially occupational goals. Once we choose a profession, the better part of our waking hours are spent at our jobs. While serving as a police officer, I had the opportunity to work with some outstanding men and women who defined excellence and professionalism. There were many highlights in my tenure as a police officer; too many to elaborate on, but several come to mind. Saving lives, administering emergency medical aid, performing CPR, reuniting a lost child with family, tending to accident victims, enforcing the law, pursuing criminals, training upcoming and in-service officers, recruiting potential police candidates, and interrogating subjects are among the more memorable aspects of my career. During specific instances whereby the justification to use deadly physical force presented itself, I was forced to draw my weapon, but fortunately, never had to succumb to using the weapon or being the target of a shooting. I am thankful to have escaped unharmed from some of the situations I encountered. I chose my father's birthday, January 2, to retire from the Suffolk County Police Department. When an officer retires he is offered the chance to keep a Class "A" dress uniform, which I did. One of my final wishes is to be laid to rest in the best suit in my closet, the Class "A" uniform. It is the suit I always wanted to wear, and it is the suit I choose to wear for eternity.

Chapter 2

Character Education: Who's That Character?

"You live for your values...you die for your beliefs."

It all began at Longwood High School, Middle Island, New York. In 1999, I had already been visiting schools as a police recruiter for approximately thirteen years. I addressed criminal justice, government, economics, and business classes, in which I discussed with students how they could educationally and socially prepare themselves for a career in law enforcement. I would then entertain questions from my audience in topics ranging from deadly force to cops and donuts. I was having lunch with teachers after several such sessions one day, and I mentioned that I would like to remain in schools after retirement. One of the educators, a Social Studies chairperson, named Dan Tomaszewski, whose classes I had been visiting for many years, suggested I consider becoming a teacher. He further commented that everything I spoke about over the years would make an excellent character education program and arranged a meeting with two of his colleagues from the school's English department. From this brainstorming meeting it was agreed upon that I would prepare a program that would be delivered to their students as part of the Humanities block of instruction which included the Social Studies/ English curriculum. I devised a program comprised of topics to include diversity, civility, character development, values clarification, civic responsibility, and violence reduction. The program is based on life experience, historic events, and uses a blend of humor and drama to take my audience on an emotional journey. Over time, I have incorporated and addressed pertinent issues brought to my attention by parents, educators, and students, thereby contouring the program for each school. As topical issues arise in our society, I utilize the events to strengthen the content of my message. My program grew when in the year 2000 New York State enacted legislation mandating schools to host character education programs aimed at reducing violence in schools. Since the inception of my character education program, I have traveled to schools from New York to California. In addition, I have developed other programs that share a common thread, namely character education.

I have been fortunate to have had positive role models in my life. My family, my educators, extended family, and friends imparted lifelong lessons in me that I have instilled in my children and now get to share with my audiences. As a young adult, I realized the lessons I received were designed to enhance my life and help me become well-rounded. The following areas of discussion are utilized to strengthen my character education messages. I consider these messages (the following terms in italicized letters) the trunk of a tree and in a given period of time the audience joins me as we build a mighty oak. *Leadership* is the key to these messages. Leaders are positive role models since they are people who others seek for guidance as they pave the way for success. Leaders are not necessarily equated to supervisors, rather they are individuals who provide solutions to problems while earning the respect of those who align themselves with them. Finally, leaders qualify the completion of goals amongst group members. I discuss the importance of *Modeling* oneself after people who are instrumental in our lives, to include family, friends, coworkers, classmates, teachers, and clergy. *Dignity,* in conjunction with honor, character, and integrity are the foundations of one's existence; preserving these traits is essential to protecting one's individual identity. *Respect* is not a given but rather a two-way street. To earn respect, you need to give it. Before you can have respect for others, you need to respect yourself. *Diversity* is an important part of life in America. Gaining an appreciation for others and their way of life enables us to co-exist in America which is coined "the melting pot of the world." *Communication* takes place in two main forms: verbal and non verbal, both of which define our daily interaction with others. Listening is an important aspect of communication and is not a passive activity but requires concentration, whereas hearing is a biological function, requiring little effort as compared to listening. Interpreting sounds into messages is what separates a good listener from one who lacks in this area. Keeping the lines of communication open improves relationships. *Profiling* is the stereotyping of a person or group based on preconceived, often inaccurate opinions related to race, religion, sex, sexual orientation, nationality, age, occupation, or physical challenge. This practice is construed by many as unfair and immoral and sometimes leads to illegal actions. *Racism* is a discriminatory act towards a person or group based on physical characteristics, including skin color, facial features, and the like. We can diminish racism and sexism in our society by becoming known among our peers as a person who will not entertain racially charged or sexual jokes and slurs. We must be ever mindful of the words we speak and in the context in which we speak them. Words are far more capable of hurt than some physical acts of violence. *Ridicule* is a practice experienced by many and occurs from something as simple as making fun of a person's name, appearance, and ethnicity. Bullying, a form of ridicule, presents itself verbally, physically, or through social networking websites. Bullying in its extreme has led people to harm themselves and others. This topical issue in our society is being addressed through education and anti-bullying campaigns in our schools and communities. Ignorance and lack of self-esteem fuel this adverse behavior on behalf of the bully. *Values* define us as people. Regardless of race, religion, sex, sexual orientation, age, occupation, ethnicity, or physical challenge we share similar values in the mere fact that we are human beings. Our values were instilled in us as children by our initial educators in life, these being parents and guardians. Agents of socialization of values also include school, religious affiliation, peers, workplace, mass media, and community. Through discretion or indiscretion, individuals can enhance or destroy their value system and everyone and everything that is important can be affected in a positive or negative way. When confronted with a moral compromise one must allude to his or her value system and adhere to it while attempting to attain a positive outcome. If we refuse to compromise, our values when making choices in life, whether personal or professional, we are apt to make the right decision. Additionally, when making choices think of how your most admired person would view your decision, and if it proved to be unacceptable how you would react to the attention it might draw. Every day we are faced with making potential life-altering decisions. Many we can control through careful planning and discipline, while other situations may be beyond our control, for example, accidents. *Destructive Decisions* are fueled by poor choices. I compare destructive decisions to a little green pea that sits atop a snow-covered mountain. As we continue to make positive choices in our lives, the pea remains frozen in place. As we make negative choices, the pea starts rolling downhill collecting snow creating an avalanche which buries us. Humans learn early in life to distinguish between doing right and doing wrong. Remaining committed to our values assists us in making a socially acceptable path, hence assisting us in living a good life.

Chapter 3

Shotgun!!!!!

"It can't happen to me."

Air, water, food, and shelter are all essential for survival. As we age and our boundaries expand, driving becomes a way of life, although many teenagers today equate it with the necessities of life. Humans possess many fears about travel, such as flying, sailing, rail, the use of bridges and tunnels, and yet one of the most dangerous of activities we undertake each day is automobile travel. Studies indicate incidents and accidents involving automobiles increase property loss, injury, and loss of life more than any other mode of travel. Additionally, the studies show that the number of fatalities among teens and young adults between the ages of fifteen and twenty-four occur as a result of automobile accidents. One of the greatest joys for parents is bringing a child into their world. As parents, we cherish every step our children take as they pass through the life stages. As our children approach their teenage years, a realization of parenthood, and in many cases, a fear sets in. Our children are now nearing adulthood and one of the rites of passage is attaining a driver's license marking the beginning of their driving career. As noted, we as parents are role models for our children. As their initial educators, we instill their values and teach them how to differentiate right from wrong. By the time our children are of age to drive, they have been observing our driving habits for at least fifteen years. Children model themselves after those closest in their lives. This is also true when it comes to driving. If we as parents speed, ignore traffic control devices, engage our mobile phones while operating a motor vehicle, drive under the influence of alcohol and drugs, or disregard our states' vehicle and traffic laws without being penalized by the justice system, our children may perceive this as acceptable behavior. In fact, the first time our children commit any of these offenses or breach any of the laws in the Vehicle and Traffic Law Book (VTL), it could be the last. If everyone drove according to the VTL we would all be perfect drivers living in a perfect driving world. Unfortunately, this is not a reality. It is paramount that parents and their teen drivers familiarize themselves with their state's licensing procedures, motor vehicle laws, and zero tolerance laws for driving under the influence of alcohol or mind-altering substances. Please be aware that the *blood alcohol content* (BAC) for drivers over the age of twenty-one is 0.08 percent nationwide (this reflects intoxication level), whereas those drivers under the age of twenty-one may fall into the zero tolerance category as legislated in New York state. For example, if a person under the age of twenty-one registers between .02 and .07 BAC, he is listed in this zero tolerance category and may be charged with driving under the influence (DUI). Blood, breath, urine, and saliva are measures used to indicate the presence of alcohol or other substances in the body. This classification includes *driving while impaired or intoxicated* (DWI) and *driving under the influence* (DUI), meaning any consumption of mind-altering substances in any proportion is not legal while operating a motor vehicle. Although, as parents we may have evaded consequences for our unlawful actions while driving, we never want to send the wrong messages to our children. Our wrong actions may leave lasting impressions on teen drivers particularly if we are not negatively sanctioned.

When we learn of the misfortunes of others in reference to motor vehicle accidents, it should be reinforced for everyone to lose the mindset, *"It can't happen to me."* This thought pattern could be fatal since we are taking common sense and knowledge, throwing it to the wind and increasing the probability that we can become victims of our own mistakes. As a parent, I sought professional driver training for both my children. When driving with them as a responsible parent, I continuously reinforced the rules of the road. At times, I knew I was perceived by my children as overbearing. While conducting my driver safety awareness program to student and parent audiences, I consistently impart these messages of safe driving. Simple things such as leaving yourself alternative maneuvers while driving, aiming for a panoramic view of the road, leaving adequate space between your vehicle and the one directly in front of you, utilizing all safety equipment, limiting the number of passengers in your car (dictated by individual state laws), driving while alert (not while drowsy), maintaining focus, and avoiding distractions in and out of your vehicle are important steps for safe driving. A teenager increases the risk of incident or accident with additional passengers in the car due to driver inattention. Texting, talking on cell phones, playing with sound systems, reading, reaching for objects in the car, eating and drinking, and applying make-up while driving are all contributing factors in crashes.

Smoking and interacting with passengers serve to detract the driver from the task at hand. Male teen drivers are more at risk than female teen drivers. Most fatal teenage crashes involve a teenage male driver and a teenage male passenger seated in the front passenger seat. This individual is commonly known as *"Shotgun."* The majority of teenage fatal crashes are the result of the aforementioned behaviors coupled with other risk factors which include weather conditions, driving under the influence of mind altering substances, time of day, and day of the week. For instance, driving on weekends increases the chance of a crash by a teen driver as does driving at dusk or nighttime. Further complicating these risk factors is the behavior associated with *Shotgun.*

Shotgun possesses the strongest personality of any passenger in the vehicle. Firstly, this person dominates all other riders when attaining the front seat. Secondly, *Shotgun* controls all activity inside and outside the car other than the physical control of the vehicle. This includes music selection, volume, and in some instances, he challenges the driver to test the car's speed capabilities. In many cases, *Shotgun* will convince the driver to give up the wheel, or grab the wheel from the driver in protest of the driver's reluctance to agree. Playful fighting is also exacerbated by *Shotgun*. *Shotgun* controls external factors such as encouraging the driver to observe persons or happenings outside the vehicle. These distractions, along with the incomplete maturation of one's brain through young adulthood in the areas of impulse and rationalization, compose the recipe for potential tragedy.

In an attempt to neutralize the risks mentioned, as well as the *Shotgun* influence, parents might consider placing a GPS device on the engine of the vehicle driven by their child. This device would monitor location and speed of the vehicle. Some applications can be downloaded to mobile phones which alert others that you are driving and cannot respond to text messages. The supplementation of these devices are not a violation of trust between parent and child, but more a matter of conscience for the parents. I highly recommend driver safety awareness programs for new and existing drivers. I found it necessary to create a parental awareness program in addition to the student driver awareness program. This program encourages parents to be proactive in all aspects of their child's lives and to set parameters which their teen driver will abide by.

If a violation of rules occurs, the driver should be penalized by the state, but should also have consequences bestowed upon them by the parents. Children of concerned parents tend to have fewer crashes and traffic offenses. This is why I not only address student audiences, but have tailored my program to include parent workshops on driver safety, thereby reinforcing the use of dialogue between the teen driver and parent.

When I was seventeen, I convinced my father to look at a sports car that I desperately wanted to own. He came with me one evening to a local car dealership, looked over the vehicle, listened to my best sales pitch as to why this car suited me, and abruptly stated, "Let's go." I thought he meant to go speak with the salesperson but he meant, "Let's go home." Upon exiting the dealership, I asked my father if there was a problem. His next sentence sobered me forever. He asked, "Do you know what I see when I look at that car?" I quipped, "Me driving it?" He responded, "I picture you in a closed box and just before it is lowered into the ground, your mother, sister, and I are placing a rose on top of it." He continued, "Not on my watch, kid." He was probably right. Through my programs I have come in contact with many wonderful individuals and families who have shared stories of grief and tragedy concerning driving. I refer to some of these instances during my program to highlight specific points. As mentioned previously, motor vehicle crashes are the leading cause of death among young and inexperienced drivers. In my programs, I reference the following scenarios including teens killed due to alleged speeding; one teen killed with alcohol as a contributing factor; one teen killed after losing control of the vehicle; two teens killed as a result of speeding; and five teens killed because of driver inattention. Let it be known that in all crashes mobile phone records may be secured by police or insurance investigators to determine a contributing factor in the moments leading to the accident. All cell phone records include contact made through either calling, texting, emailing, or any other use of cell phone applications. A chronological log to include time and date is maintained by the mobile phone provider and is made available to investigators upon request or subpoena, particularly when cases involve fatalities. First responders to a crash secure the scene, tend to the injured, interview witnesses, prepare reports, request tow trucks to remove vehicles, while police officers have the added and sometimes difficult responsibility of notification to next of kin. In the tragic cases of a motor vehicle fatality, police and detectives are now entrusted with the most difficult assignment, that being "The Knock On The Door." Although dreaded, officers are adept in this function, yet death notification training never fully prepares the officer for the reality he or she will face. When a family opens the door and observes a police officer who was not summoned to the home, uneasiness sets in. An officer can expect any reaction once the news of a fatality involving a family member is delivered, including denial and mistrust. After stating the name of the party involved, it is anticipated that the aggrieved family member will acknowledge the death prior to the officer actually verbalizing the message. This helps to alleviate denial experienced by family members. Sympathy, empathy and compassion are vital attributes on behalf of the officer in the delivery of this news. Oft times the officers bearing this news spend countless hours with the family, comforting and consoling them in this time of tragedy. This is a knock on the door that no family ever wants to receive, especially in the case of teenage deaths. It is not the natural order to outlive our children and when it occurs it turns lives upside down forever. Family members have expressed to me that nothing in their lives has the same meaning after the loss of a loved one. Holidays and other celebrations fall short of what they once were. Time does not heal the loss of a child. I beg teenagers to think before they act in all aspects of their lives, especially when operating a motor vehicle and how everyone and everything can be changed in an instant through poor choices. When a teenage death occurs, the news spreads far and wide. I recently heard that the Pope included in a sermon at The Vatican the names of five teenagers who lost their lives in a car accident here in the United States in the fall of 2011. When a teen death occurs, hundreds of students from many school districts attend the funeral proceedings. As this news is vastly distributed, teens unite and gather as a show of strength for the family. I have attended many such wakes and funerals and pray that I will never have to attend another.

I ask that *Shotgun* be a positive influence and leader. I request that he or she serve as an additional set of eyes and ears while maintaining a positive force within the vehicle. I further ask *Shotgun* to ensure that the driver is sober from any substance, legal or illegal, and is not drowsy while driving, or suffers any other condition that could compromise the safe operation of the vehicle.

Shotgun should be prepared to assume the role of designated driver should these elements exist. *Shotgun*, as a positive force, is also entrusted with maintaining the discipline among all passengers. I also ask all passengers if they find themselves in a dangerous situation, to step up and do their best to convince the driver to correct his actions to avoid a potential disaster. If this negotiating fails, do everything within your power to convince the driver to stop the vehicle, relinquish the keys, and allow the passengers to exit. Teenagers and young adults should have an agreement with their parents or guardian that when in a dangerous situation they can call them for safe passage home, no questions asked. This does not condone unacceptable behavior. The next morning when the smoke clears, those who summoned their parents will now communicate as to how they got into the dangerous situation and what they will do in the future to avoid a similar circumstance. The parent in this agreement also pledges to their young adult that if they find themselves in a dangerous situation they too will seek safe transportation home. Drivers keep in mind that your passengers, regardless of age, are the children of loving and caring parents. I beg you on bended knee to lose the mindset, "It can't happen to me." Stay safe....please.

Chapter 4

The Class of Life (COL)

"Remember to tell those in your life who you love, 'I LOVE YOU' and with those words comes a hug and a kiss."

As per the "Topic" page on my website, *The Class of Life (COL)* is described as follows, "We all enroll in the *Class of Life.* Why do some of us fare better in this course than others? Through humor, similes and verbal demonstration we learn the do's and don'ts of success. Engaging in small role play and "how to" behavior demonstrates that certain body language and verbal expression will lead participants into a life of fulfilling their goals. Scenarios depicting daily actions show students how the slightest attention to detail can make the greatest difference. Interpersonal skills and life skills are addressed and reinforced. Learn how to recognize your potential by not taking anything for granted." Over the years, many schools have brought this hypothetical, innovative, and interactive program to their students. While most suited for transitioning students from high school to college and from college to career, I have conducted this program before a wide range of audiences. An initial order of business in this class will require each student to sign a pledge to abstain from alcohol, tobacco, and any other legal or illegal mind-altering or physically compromising substances.

Getting people to understand the way we think, speak, and carry ourselves is important in accomplishing our goals. *The Class of Life* emphasizes promptness, neatness in preparing materials, professional dress, our use of vocabulary, with special emphasis on utilizing words to include "Please, Thank You, You're Welcome, and May I," while eliminating slang words such as "Yea, Nah and Yo" and replacing them with "Yes and No, Ma'am and Sir." Common courtesies such as the holding of doors for others, giving up a seat for someone else, and using the above words appropriately will serve to further enhance one's overall demeanor. Additional etiquette training is provided to give students the advantage of displaying the proper behaviors when at a table for dinner or formal gathering. Table-setting preparation is a focal point in the etiquette section of the *"COL"* as is maintaining one's personal living quarters in an orderly fashion.

Defining and discussing personal values and occupational goals are key components of the program. Once defined, guest speakers will be invited to class to explain how they educationally and socially prepared themselves for their chosen profession.   Regular visitors to class will include parents and guardians to strengthen the line of communication among students and their families. Students will have a clear understanding of how education and social decisions do not always go hand in hand and realize that the level of education one achieves cannot compensate for poor moral choices, no matter how high that level may be. Field trips are used for practical purposes in the class. For instance, these trips will bring students to financial institutions to teach them how to open financial accounts, how to balance a checkbook, the importance of remitting bill payments as time prescribes; students will visit various venues throughout the community to prepare them how to launder clothes, and how to make change when purchasing items. A trip to the local police agencies, jails, and courts will provide insight into our legal system while giving students a prospective on consequences of poor choices they may make as young adults in society. One of the final field trips will include a visit to an undertaker for a better understanding of the final phase of life. Students will be encouraged to recommend future field trips that will bring forth more practical life experience.

An additional topic provided in the *COL* is *leadership.* Those who display leadership qualities will be empowered to step up when confronted with bullying or any perceived injustice. These leaders will be well-versed in handling and reporting such incidences. The idea is to promote proactive behavior among all students and to get them to understand how to properly react to negative situations. Our leaders will guide others to the right path fully understanding that if "They talk the talk, they must walk the walk." Throughout the curriculum, developing and enhancing leadership and interpersonal skills, while learning how to appreciate diversity and gain acceptance towards oneself and others, is continuously reiterated.

Through mock sessions, each student will graduate the class with the knowledge of how to prepare a professional resume, the confidence to utilize public speaking, and the tools needed to conduct themselves fluently on a job interview. Any use of inappropriate slurs or jokes alluding to racism, sexism, vulgarity, crudeness, or rudeness will be grounds for immediate expulsion from the class. Each day an appropriate joke or humorous story will be delivered by a different student. My dad often told me he missed out socially because he didn't dance. So each day we will begin the class with humor and contemporary dance. Knowledge and performance of my innovative dance, *The Paulie,* will be incorporated into the curriculum. Songs depicting human condition will be used to illustrate and highlight life experiences pertinent to the students in the class. The use of cell phones, mobile devices, and explicitly disrespectful or suggestive apparel will be prohibited. Provocative clothing should be avoided while all students adhere to the school dress code as defined. All school rules will be followed in accordance with the code of conduct as mandated by each respective learning institution. Parents and guardians will be called upon to participate in any phase of education by utilizing real life experience and knowledge to further the curriculum. These people will also be called upon to prepare their favorite family recipes for the class to share. Herein, cultural awareness is gained through food, music, and dance of varying ethnicities. As

COL students come to celebrate rites of passage such as spring break, prom, banquet, and graduation, it is entrusted upon them to initiate, in conjunction with school administration and parents, mandated awareness programs regarding the responsibility of the school, parents, and students outlining protocol for these events. A signed contractual agreement between the aforementioned parties that the student attended the awareness workshop with parent, and fully understands the rules and consequences of violating protocol, will be required at the end of the program to allow access into each event.

The ultimate goal in the *COL* is to enable participants to reach maximum potential while considering the aspects in their lives that are most important, while never compromising their value system. The final examination in the *COL* will be the toughest ever endured in any curriculum in any level of education. The examination will test the ability of the student as he or she goes forward in life. If one leads a morally sound, productive life that individual receives an *A+*. Conversely, a life based on ethical indiscretion will most likely earn a failing grade. The choice is yours.

Chapter 5

The Devil Made Me Do It: The Demons

"A gang, simply defined, is a group of people with like interests and cause that band together to accomplish same."

The **Demons** are the oldest, most deadly gang in our society. My father, the greatest man I knew, was killed by a member of this gang which has several subdivisions. Each tier is responsible for destroying another human life through devastation, destruction, and perseverance. The gang members in each sector create havoc while leaving a path of destruction equal to a that of a tornado. The subdivision that contributed to my father's passing was the *"tobacco"* demon. Years ago, prior to the awareness of the dangers of cigarette smoke, the tobacco demon was popular and recruited members at early ages. Although this demon still recruits at early ages today, it has somewhat subsided in its popularity. Unfortunately, tobacco is sold in mass quantities and remains rampant among the youth in our society. Once the tobacco demon enters a person's life, it becomes an addiction to reckon with. The addiction is one of a physical nature since nicotine, the active ingredient in tobacco, is a stimulant and once inhaled gives the user a "lift." The elevated feeling lasts only seconds to minutes, thereby causing the person to crave more. As time progresses, the need for more nicotine increases. This tolerance effect is what leads people to succumb to the ill effects of tobacco smoking. The combination of tars, other additives, and the smoke produced by lighting a cigarette, is a deadly storm which eventually will attack the lungs, heart, and other bodily organs. Studies have indicated the negative consequences that tobacco has on nonsmokers and the environment. The second-hand smoke, as it is commonly referred to, has been named in many cancer-related diagnoses and has contributed to countless cases of heart disease and stroke. So ask yourself, "Why smoke if it is so bad for one's health?" The answer partially lies with the social realm of tobacco and the need to feel accepted by peers as they experiment with the product. The issues at hand are the damages caused by tobacco, the economic impact on society, and the long term results of its consumption. Thus, the use of tobacco, whether inhaled or chewed, according to the medical profession, is highly addictive, dangerous, and costly in the long run. Costs for insurance claims rise, hospital visits climb, sick days and loss of wages are incurred, while death is the ultimate loss due to tobacco dependence. Before there were warnings on cigarette packaging, my dad used to hold up a cigarette, point his thumb to his chest, and tell me, "If I thought this was good for you, I would buy you a carton a day and sit with you to make sure you smoked every cigarette in the carton. But I'll be honest with you, son, I think this is killing me." And it did. My father died of a smoking-related condition.

The second subdivision of the demons is *"alcohol."* Alcohol is the most widely used substance among teens and those in the college years. Alcohol is classified as a legal drug when used in accordance with documented legislation. Each state in the country is mandated to adhere to federal laws with respect to alcohol sales and consumption. For instance, the legal age to acquire and consume alcohol is twenty-one. All states enforce DWI laws and punish in accordance with set standards if violated. Since alcohol is widely accepted in society for rites of passage ceremonies and other social occasions, it is used with much frequency. Alcohol is classified as one of the most habit-forming drugs here and abroad. However, each society defines its norms differently when referring to alcohol use. In America, the Blood Alcohol Content (BAC) for legal intoxication is .08. If we were to travel abroad, we might find that there is no BAC measurement as each society views alcohol and its effects differently. In the United States, we often fail to recognize alcohol as a drug, yet it is one of the most powerful mind-altering substances abused. Alcohol is a guest at so many functions and is responsible for death on our roadways, sickness and disease, and has been a culprit in the irrational decisions that we often make when under the influence. These decisions lead to fatal mistakes and once they are implemented there is no way to turn back. Alcohol exposure begins at an early age determined by a society's norms and values. The legal drinking age has been vastly ignored and the addiction rate concerning alcohol is in epidemic proportion. Despite the rehabilitation services available to alcoholics, the relapse rate remains high simply because once addicted, the person faces a difficult battle for abstinence. One does not lose the status of alcohol addiction. However, one exists in a struggle to keep this demon away. Alcohol is often considered one of the most sought after drugs in our society, yet remains as an entity in itself, thereby warranting its own discussion in textbooks, literature, and public forums addressing drug use. The following information will refer to drugs that are legal and illegal and are either abused or misused.

The third subdivision of the demons is *"drugs." (For this upcoming section, I consulted my editor, Nancy DiMonte, who has an extensive background in substance abuse education and awareness).* Drugs are classified into several categories ranging from antidepressants and pain suppressors, to tranquilizers and mood elevators. No matter the choice of drug, people need to bear in mind that all drugs, legal, or otherwise, have the potential of causing side effects or serious reactions. In addition, using two drugs or more simultaneously can pose unanticipated side effects or even death. Drinking coffee will not negate the effects of alcohol, as believed. Although alcohol is a depressant and caffeine is a stimulant, the caffeine in coffee serves to awaken a person but does not lessen the state of intoxication from the alcohol. Drugs are prescribed for specific reasons. However, in our society we have taken these prescriptions and used them for experimentation and recreation. Few, if any drugs have ever been solely invented for recreation except possibly alcohol, which is used as a prop for religious celebrations, weddings, graduations, and many life stage milestones. The sale of drugs commonly found in household medicine cabinets has skyrocketed. Parents need to be mindful that drugs not in use should be discarded through methods legislated by each state. For example, no drug should be discarded into garbage bins, septic systems, or commercial trash receptacles. Some local police departments will accept the drugs for proper disposal. There are many venues in which to purchase drugs for recreational use. Some include school grounds, bars, and social establishments. However, drugs can be obtained through internet websites, "pharming" parties where various drugs are contributed and up for grabs by attendees, or simply by word of mouth. Drugs are often introduced to a person in their purest form at the onset of experimentation. As time passes, and the user becomes more tolerant of the substance, he or she will be in the market for more. But with each subsequent purchase, the price is adjusted to reflect the economy. When supply exceeds demand, the price of the sought after drug is lowered and when demand exceeds supply, the price is raised. In fact, the drug becomes "laced" or lacks purity or consistency when supply is limited. Drugs sold illegally are often cut with toxic chemicals that will ultimately cause harm, or if ingested in high amounts, death. Drug trends reflect society's supply and demand at any given time. The preferred choices of drugs today based on the current trends are alcohol, marijuana, and many of the prescription drugs found in household medicine cabinets. Some of these include pain medications which are mostly synthetic. Among these are *Vicoden (hydrocodone bitartrate) and Oxycodone (oxycodone hydrochloride)* which are included in the classification of opiates or opioids. Heroin is also included in this classification, yet is not typically found in medicine cabinets as it is not legally prescribed. It is in high demand but easily obtained through street sales at a price that is affordable to many users. Its supply is ample, although it is cut with unknown additives, thereby driving the price down while raising the quantity available. Heroin has obtained national attention in recent years and has spiraled out of control amongst teens and young adults. Another widespread trend is the use of alprazolam or *Xanax* as referred to by the brand name. This is prescribed for the relief of anxiety and is dosed according to severity of condition or emotional need. In other words, the dosages are often at the discretion of the doctor's interpretation of the patient's description of the problem. Since doctors may need to rely much upon patient recount, the doctor may prescribe for a given situation after a reasonable assessment is made. However, patients may take it upon themselves to adjust the dosage as they fluctuate in anxiety or face a particularly anxious scenario. So it is important to monitor the patient's emotional health while taking anti-anxiety medication to insure that the correct dose is being utilized. Keeping scheduled follow up visits with trained mental health professionals is something that the patient must be cognizant of. As dependency develops, some users attempt to circumvent the system. If a doctor deems that a patient is not a candidate for a refill of the drug, the patient often becomes agitated. When a doctor declines to write another prescription, patients will seek out a new physician who does not know them in the hopes that a new prescription will be written. This "doctor shopping" has become an escalating problem in a society where these anti-anxiety drugs are widely accepted. Said drugs are placed in a stricter category when prescribing. Still, these are dispensed for even the slightest cases of anxiety and carry huge consequences if misused. The addiction rate is substantial. Therefore, the disbursement on prescriptions needs to be monitored more closely. Some states have instituted a more refined database for cross reference of prescriptions for a single patient, thereby possibly decreasing the availability of the drug to a patient. The effectiveness of the database should be revisited and adhered to in order to curtail the unnecessary use and distribution of narcotics or drugs in question.

Marijuana (a stimulant) is a popular choice of drug in all parts of the world. It is legal in some countries but illegal in others. In the United States, there has been continuous debate about legalizing or decriminalizing this drug for various reasons. In the New York State Penal Law, there are four categories of offenses, namely *infractions, violations, misdemeanors, and felonies.* Of the four offenses, two are crimes, including misdemeanors and felonies. Several years ago through New York State legislation, possession of marijuana in certain amounts for personal use in a private environment dropped from the misdemeanor category to a violation of law. Any public use, display, or sale of marijuana in any amount is upgraded to the criminal level. Sale of marijuana is more serious a crime than possession. Quantity plays a part in how the legal system will proceed. To further clarify, the aforementioned offenses include fines and or imprisonment upon conviction. PLEASE NOTE THAT DECRIMINALIZATION IS NOT THE SAME AS LEGALIZATION!!!! The active ingredient in marijuana is *THC* which stands for *Tetrahydrocannabinol*. This is the psychoactive ingredient found in the cannabis plant and has been recognized in the medical community for some healing properties and analgesic (pain reducing) effects. However, many studies have been restricted due to legislation prohibiting its use and distribution. Other studies show contraindications to include decrease in concentration, delayed reflexes, short-term memory loss, and altered vision, hearing, and smell. The increase in appetite has not been linked to a keen sense of taste but rather to a stimulation in the appetite sensors in the brain. THC in its purest form has not been cited definitively in the death of any humans. However, toxicity involving fatality can occur from smoking marijuana if the substance is laced with lethal ingredients. While these deaths are relatively rare, they should be mentioned. In addition, deaths due to accidents involving impaired driving due to marijuana are on the rise.

The leader of the *Demons* lies in the subdivision of drugs. The leader will be referred to as *Crack/Cocaine.* Some whom I've arrested while in the warrant section of the police department have claimed that this drug is a "one time experiment and a lifetime addiction." One such individual claimed, "The first high I attained from crack was the highest I had ever experienced." In a never-ending attempt, he strives to reach that high again, but continuously falls short. This drug has cost him his wife, home, job, and physical attributes for a fleeting high. This intense elation lasts only from 8 to 10 minutes upon which the craving for more overtakes the mind. The frequency needed to satisfy the user may become cost prohibitive. Moreover, the lack of financial means does not stop the user from figuring out a way to secure the drug. Therefore, the user often resorts to criminal activity in order to satisfy this demon. Similarly, cocaine generates incredible heights of elation. This drug is responsible for one feeling grandiose, while creating a false sense of heightened awareness. The user believes that he is able to concentrate and develop an acute use of his senses. In fact, this is a misconception. The stimulation from this drug is so potent that it creates this misconstrued perception of self. While withdrawing from these drugs does not bear the same meaning as withdrawal from opiates, the substances can take their toll on the body physically. These drugs command more mental withdrawal and can possibly be stopped on a "cold turkey" basis. There are few serious physical complications from withdrawal. Mentally, the drugs pose the greatest risks of relapse. Both crack and cocaine have tremendous power in deceiving the psyche. When the drug gets into your heart and mind, it is only a matter of time before it consumes your soul.

The fourth subdivision of the demons is *"gambling."* Although not directly fatal, it has been known that this addiction could lead to one's demise since it is often a prelude to other demons mentioned. When one possesses one demon, he often displays the behavior of a concurrent demon. Gambling can occur in any venue that allows for waging bets, illegally or legally in gambling houses such as casinos, betting parlors, office football pools, racetracks, and even on the internet. Television has been a huge promoter of gambling as poker tournaments are glorified and viewed by millions. Lottery and scratch-off tickets are purchased from hundreds of convenience stores and vendors across the country. But in reality, the "house" or sponsor of the games wins. Very often, a compulsive gambler possesses the characteristics of an addictive personality much like the one who abuses alcohol, drugs, and tobacco. One or more of these demons, combined with gambling, can be the recipe for disaster. The gambling demon is no less addictive than the previous three mentioned subdivisions. The gambling demon goes right to your soul. No matter how much you win, you can't satisfy this demon. For instance, any losses accrued through gambling are grossly understated since the gambler unknowingly lays down more than what is returned. When the gambler gets a return, however small it may be, the excitement overtakes the truth. This pattern continues, thereby giving the gambler a false sense of power and excitement. This leads to the compulsion and inability to stop. The danger lies with the fact that the gambler will eventually draw from savings accounts and other income sources until he depletes the cash flow. In order to gain additional cash, the gambler may eventually resort to irrational means in which to obtain the money to continue the obsession. The games are only a small part of the formula. In actuality, the gambler feels a heightened sense just by winning, even if it is only a small amount. The demon is expensive, causing the participant to feel a sense of powerlessness when cash is lost. This diminished sense of self is often times the path to destruction. Gambling is classified as a disorder when it interferes with normal life activities. One only has to look at the grand style of a casino and ask this simple question, "Who wins?" The odds are stacked in favor of the house. Gambling facilities would not survive in a losing environment. Not everyone who gambles is possessed by this demon. Recreational gambling is enjoyed by many who draw a line in the sand and are not compelled to overstep their boundaries. An occasional trip to cities that host gambling are enjoyed by many casual gamblers. Patrons of stores carrying games of chance tickets are categorized as recreational gamblers if they are not consumed with the cards and do not enter into debt to continue purchasing the cards.

In our society the word "gang" carries a negative connotation. Simply defined, a gang is a group of three or more members who share common goals. A gang is a type of subculture that is bonded together to accomplish a culture of its own. This is not always abnormal, but when the gang goes against the dominant culture, it becomes a counterculture, thus stereotyping gangs as illegal and undesirable. So we need to establish our place in society and choose to be a part of a productive subculture that benefits us by teaching us to appreciate other cultures within the society. Positive subcultures include police, firefighters, military, educators, health care providers, and select fraternities, amongst many others. Members of these groups will often refer to themselves as "the gang" in an endearing way.

Tobacco, alcohol, drugs, and gambling are only four subdivisions of the demons. There are other demons that afflict people not mentioned within this text. Once afflicted, a person can seek therapy, rehabilitation, or in some cases, "cold turkey--immediate cessation of behavior, " is viable. Regardless of the affliction, once the demon is assessed, a lifetime of abstinence becomes the only option towards normalcy. Addiction is a strong characteristic of any demon and curing addiction is not typical as most addictions are treatable but not curable. The primary goal of dealing with addiction should be to keep the behavior suppressed and to control temptation. Addicts are counseled in doing so. If an individual seeks help, I encourage him or her to investigate the many avenues in which to turn. Private and public agencies can be utilized and many insurance companies may provide coverage, full or partial, in the counseling process. In every case, controlling demons is an uphill battle that escalates if unattended to. As we are not cured of demons, we can keep them from rearing their ugly heads with the proper support and guidance of professionals, family, friends, and educators. One should always remember that the chances of demonic behavior increase once a person has experienced one of the subdivisions. One subdivision of the demons is often a gateway to another.

In an attempt to further enlighten our readers on how the realities of substance abuse play a role in everything we do, we interviewed a substance abuser and got his perspective on addiction and its consequences. We were faced with where to place the forthcoming interview in this book and decided that while drug addiction is a demon, it also involves ethical choices. Therefore, we placed this interview and the others in Chapter 5 in the hopes to connect drug use and its impact on society. Following the interview of the recovering user, we gathered interviews with those whose professional and personal lives are affected by users. These people included police, parents, siblings, and counselors.

All gave a different perspective on the user's impact on society, but all concluded that addiction is harmful to society at large. As you read each interview, bear in mind the emotional consequences each person goes through when dealing with substance abuse. Realize that while each one has a specific role in the control of this problem, they all work in unison to hopefully eradicate the problem or keep it from proliferating.

The Interview

The following is a real-life experience. The subject of this interview volunteered his story in the hopes that it would inspire some to seek help when they feel the need to. He is recovering from addiction to prescription pain medications. To protect the identity of the person we interviewed we will use a pseudonym. We will refer to him as "Jimmy." Jimmy is a twenty-two year old male living on Long Island. The interview was done in the conventional "question and answer" method with some discussion added at the end.

Question 1: How old are you?

Response: *Twenty-two years old.*

Question 2: Where do you live?

Response: *Commack, New York.*

Question 3: Discuss your employment history. Include present employment.

Response: *I have had around thirteen different jobs. I worked in several fast food establishments, factory shipping and receiving, a pharmacy, business brokerage firm, and volunteered with the local fire department as an EMT. I currently work as a server at a local chain restaurant.*

Question 4: Are you a college graduate?

Response: *I am currently attending a college on Long Island which is part of the State University of New York. I am a matriculated student and am gradually transitioning into a full time curriculum.*

Question 5: Do you have both parents? Are they married or divorced? How many siblings do you have?

Response: *I live with both of my parents who are married. I have one older brother and two older sisters.*

Question 6: When did you begin using illegal substances?

Response: *I was only seventeen when I began using drugs.*

Question 7: What was your first experimental illegal drug?

Response: *My first encounter with illegal substances was marijuana. I first started drinking since it was easy to obtain alcohol. I drank once every two weeks and vodka was my number one choice.*

Question 8: Do you currently use alcohol?

Response: *No. I do not drink alcohol since I am recovering and it could impair my judgment.*

Question 9: What were the circumstances surrounding your first encounter with illegal drugs?

Response: *I would go to parties where everyone would be drinking. My friends and I then began to smoke pot and it became a daily ritual. We smoked constantly, sometimes over twenty-four hour periods of time! My friends supplied me with marijuana for the first time. I believe that marijuana was the gateway for my desire to move on to more potent drugs. After a while when I continuously smoked marijuana, I found that the drug had little effect on me. I was not satisfied with the high I got from smoking. I experimented with the opiates to gain more momentum.*

Question 10: Do you smoke cigarettes?

Response: *Seldom*

Question 11: Did you spend any time in the hospital due to drugs?

Response: *I never ended up in a hospital because of using drugs.*

Question 12: Did you spend time as an outpatient or inpatient in a treatment facility due to substance abuse? How long? When? What made you enter a facility? Are you on withdrawal medication?

Response: *I am currently an outpatient at a rehabilitation center close to home. I visit there once a month. I see a therapist twice monthly. The psychotherapist visits include individual and group counseling. I began treatment April 4, 2012 after I was forced to do so by my parents. I was economically unable to support myself. My parents gave me an ultimatum which allowed me only two options to choose from. These were to either seek rehabilitation and treatment or to leave their home. I chose treatment.*

I entered the facility for excessive use of Oxycodone which I obtained through various sources. It took me nine months to reach a dosage of 240 mg 8x daily. I crushed and snorted the drug. I never tried heroin although people who use Oxycodone often use heroin. I paid upwards of $30.00 a pill, sometimes paying as much as $240.00 while on a binge. I rationalized the use of these pain medications since Vicoden was prescribed for my tonsillectomy.

My parents recognized a problem as I kept an ashy appearance, vomited at times, and suffered visible weight loss. My overall wellness had been quite compromised and was apparent. My parents were alerted to my using as I would steal money from them to support my habit. I went to an extreme when I pawned my parents' wedding rings. I displayed poor judgment when I operated a motor vehicle under the influence.

I was put on a regimen of Suboxone to aid in the withdrawal of the Oxycodone. I currently take Suboxone once daily, but have gradually decreased the dosage which will allow me to wean off of it safely and effectively. Soon I will not be using this medication as the dosage is minimal, and I have remained drug-free.

Question 13: Describe your experience in the rehabilitation facility.

Response: *When I feel temptation I look towards the support staff which is most necessary in helping me to resist using.*

I couldn't deal with the many emotions I was feeling. The rehabilitation has helped me with the emotional roller coaster I sometimes encounter. My experience in rehabilitation is very positive.

Question 14: Have you ever been associated with a crime due to drug use?

Response: *I was caught stealing money from my parents to support my addiction. Additionally, I stole from my workplace whenever I had the opportunity to do so. The blame was always put on someone else, and I was never arrested.*

Question 15: What does the future hold for you?

Response: *My first priority to ensure my future is to stay clean. I would like to educate others on behalf of substance abuse. This is one way in which I can give back to society. I envision that my future also holds my having a functional family.*

Question 16: How will you insure that you will remain clean of substances?

Response: *I read books and magazines to keep off substances. I also find that meditation helps me in the process of healing. I feel that I need to increase my physical activity since I do not spend enough time exercising. I consider myself an average eater;*

I try to maintain a healthy diet but could use improvement in this area. Physically, I am in decent shape and will continue to schedule yearly well visits with my doctor. Currently, I feel physically and emotionally awesome. I am confident that I will not "fall off the wagon." I am now enrolled in college with the hopes of earning a degree.

Question 17: What advice would you give to a person who is struggling with addiction?

Response: *I would tell them "Don't believe others, go with your gut instincts." If you don't trust someone then trust yourself and follow your own heart. Using drugs causes one to compromise his or her thought process, thereby altering ethical conscience. My suggestion is that if you experiment with something you feel you shouldn't have, seek help immediately instead of continuing forward. Implement the best judgment you can and seek out positive role models for help.*

The above questions were posed by the editor of the book. They were planned well in advance of the interview. After these were answered, I then spontaneously developed questions to complete the interview. This became very emotional for all involved since Jimmy was expressing his innermost feelings which affected us all. The following is the second set of questions posed:

Question 18: How do you feel about the legalization of marijuana for recreational use?

Response: *I believe that marijuana is a gateway drug and do not agree with the legalization of it.*

Question 19: What socioeconomic class best describes your family? Describe your family life.

Response: *We would be classified as an upper middle class family. We were a loving, connected, and functional family. I was raised as a Catholic, although today I do not fully practice the faith.*

Question 20: How would you describe your level of self-esteem while growing up and at present?

Response: *I had a high self-esteem which was affected by the addiction, but I am regaining a stronger sense of self. I was surrounded by many friends, had a good childhood, and shared like interests with peers, to include soccer and paintball. I never considered myself popular, but I got along with all crowds of kids. I would have considered myself as a leader and very influential. In fact, I was so influential that I regrettably led a friend down the path of drug abuse. (This is when Jimmy left the room to gain composure). To this day I feel great remorse for having done so. I have had to relinquish many acquaintances since their involvement with drugs could drag me down. I have to reestablish relationships that will be beneficial to me when leading a drug-free life.*

Question 21: Have you ever been bullied?

Response: *I can honestly say I was never bullied or threatened, but sadly I admit that I have bullied others. I had the opportunity to make amends when a person I bullied years ago came into my place of employment, and I apologized for my past actions.*

Question 22: What age do you think you will live to be?

Response: *I never cared about it, or thought about it.*

Question 23: Did you ever experience suicidal thoughts or tendencies while on drugs?

Response: *No. I never contemplated suicide.*

Question 24: Did you think about the consequences of your driving a motor vehicle while under the influence?

Response: *I usually stayed in one place while on drugs. I rarely operated a vehicle when I was high. Sometimes I would be alone in my world and did not venture out. I knew that it could hurt others to drive while under the influence, but the reason I stayed off the road was because I just wanted to relish the high while remaining stationary.*

Question 25: Do you plan to have a family of your own some day?

Response: *Yes I would like to marry and have children.*

Question 26: If you had a weapon and wanted to confiscate pain pills, do you think your addiction would have perpetuated the use of your weapon to obtain the pills?

Response: *It is hard to say, but I hope not. Yet I couldn't account for being irrational while on opiates. Thankfully, this scenario was not a part of my addiction as it is common in many others.*

The interview ends with a quote from Jimmy:

"The instant you put a chemical in your brain, you are no longer the person you were."

Post Interview Discussion: January 15, 2013

Today was my final dose of Suboxone. Since the interview my life is better in every respect. Work is more enjoyable, my relationship with my parents and family is better, my relationship with my girlfriend is better. My education has finally gained momentum, and I am on track to get a degree come this fall. All of these are a direct result of my sobriety. At first, it is hard to see the fruits of all the labor involved in sobriety. Now that I can see how life is so much better it is a new found motivation to stay clean.

When you are in active addiction you see the world with a sort of tunnel vision. Sobriety is the gift of clarity; now I no longer see life with tunnel vision. I can see the big picture. May 5, 2013--As of this writing, I am clean for one year, am contemplating a career in social work, and believe that I will remain abstinent since I intend to attend current and future NA meetings. Those who stay on course are those who stick with the program.

The Interview II

This second interview was granted to us by a couple from a suburb in The United States that experienced life with a son who succumbed to substance abuse. His addiction led him to rehabilitation and a whole new existence for himself and his family. While the interview took about two hours to complete, it became apparent during this time that the subjects of the discussion were visiting a very sensitive topic. All the questions were answered with as much accuracy as could be provided and an emotional tone remained throughout since these parents were reminded of their battle with their son's addiction. The family consists of the parents and two sons, both in their twenties. The younger son is currently in treatment for substance addiction. Pseudonyms were applied throughout the interview to protect the privacy of the participants.

Question 1: Describe the relationship with your son prior to his drug use.

Response: *The relationship was good. He was a bit distant as a son, but we felt that our son lived in a secret world. Outside of that world we believed he was gentle and caring. The relationship overall was good amongst all in the family.*

Question 2: How long had your son been using?

Response: *Approximately four years beginning in senior year of high school. After high school, he attended a four-year college for about a period of one year. He then transferred to a local community college where he attained a two-year degree. During his attendance at the first college, he began his road to heavy drug use. It continued throughout his remaining years in school.*

Question 3: What substances have been used by your son? Which were used most frequently?

Response: *To the best of our knowledge, he began with legal drugs, including alcohol and cigarettes, which led to the experimentation with marijuana. We believed that the marijuana was the gateway to his use of cocaine, pain killers, crack, and heroin. Our son started to snort heroin and then resorted to shooting up. Patterns changed with choice of drugs, but the usage became more frequent until the abuse of heroin necessitated a regime in rehabilitation.*

Question 4: What was the first drug ever used by your son?

Response: *We are not entirely sure, but to the best of our knowledge we don't think he was a heavy user of alcohol. He drank socially and as stated before, we think he began using pot in the beginning.*

Question 5: Does your son currently use alcohol or smoke cigarettes?

Response: *Yes, he smokes cigarettes, but must abstain from alcohol since it is not permitted in the rehabilitation process.*

Question 6: How long has your son been in treatment?

Response: *Our son has been a resident of a treatment facility for approximately one year. He recently received recognition of his achievement of his sobriety for that time period. He will remain a resident after the graduation in June when he will begin a transition period.*

Question 7: Has your relationship with your son improved or deteriorated since the onset of rehabilitation?

Response: *The relationship has been amazing. The last year has created a whole new relationship for me as a father with my son. As a mother, I feel renewed and a sense of a more open and communicative relationship. At this time our relationship with our son is excellent.*

Question 8: How did your son become admitted to a facility for treatment?

Response: *In the fall of 2012, our son's life was spiraling out of control due to his substance abuse. He requested to go to detoxification after he sustained substantial injuries from a beating by an unknown assailant. With few hospitals offering detox services, we went to a county medical center with a reputation for fine drug detoxification procedures. After a five-day stay, we researched several treatment options and our son volunteered, reluctantly, to attend the current facility. He is now classified as a long-term resident, and his length of stay will be determined by his progress.*

Question 9: What physical changes did you notice in your son after the onset of drug use?

Response: *We noticed a change in sleep habits along with a noticeable weight loss. His eyes appeared sunken with dark circles under them. He seemed ashy. In addition, he looked unkempt.*

Question 10: What mental/emotional changes did you notice?

Response: *Our son was moody, irritable, short-tempered, became stand-offish, evasive, and angry. He lied to us on many occasions. He was secretive and shirked responsibility. He eventually stopped working and was living in cars. He crashed cars and blacked out. It was chaotic and insane!*

Question 11: Did any violence occur during your son's drug use?

Response: *No violent acts were committed towards us or anyone else that we are aware of. He did not in any way threaten the family.*

Question 12: Were any crimes committed during his chemical dependency?

Response: *There were crimes committed and scams that were completely out of character. Even being sent to jail for a short time did not seem to alter this behavior. The drug culture had turned him into someone with no regard for ethics or morality. This was evidenced by the fact that he resorted to stealing from our family.*

Question 13: How was your son's addiction funded?

Response: *At first he used money he earned on his job as a cook in a restaurant. As his dependency worsened, he stole cash from the family store, pawned jewelry, and accomplished an accumulation of cash by opening legitimate credit card accounts, purchasing and pawning goods. He did not pay the credit companies when due and racked up a huge amount of debt.*

Question 14: How have you been instrumental in the recovery of your son?

Response: *Treatment consumes every part of our lives. We visit and support his efforts as much as we can. There was a time when we turned to medication to deal with our own stress from it all. We lost sleep, could not eat and sought therapy. Yet we remained hopeful and did what was needed step-by-step to help ourselves and our son to see a way through this.*

Question 15: Were there any relapses during his stay in the facility?

Response: *Thankfully, there were no relapses, but our son did leave the facility against regulations one time after he started the program. His reason for leaving was misguided, and there were consequences for his action. Since that incident he has remained consistent with no violations of agreement to treatment.*

Question 16: How was his brother affected by the addiction?

Response: *Our older son was angry over the grief that we incurred because of the substance abuse.*

He was furious and remained cautious about reviving a relationship with his brother. Both sons have a good relationship today, and the oldest boy supports his younger brother fully.

Question 17: What are the hopes for the future of your son and of yourselves?

Response: *We take one day at a time. Our son is headed towards a four-year degree. He probably won't return to his old position in his industry as the environment is not conducive to his sobriety. He could own his own business one day, and most of all, we can put so much of the past behind us.*

Question 18: What advice would you give to other parents who are faced with this problem?

Response: *If you notice something out of the ordinary then go with your gut instinct and follow through. Investigate your concerns. Don't deny a problem. Do not be an enabler. Limit the flow of cash, even if it means closing bank accounts and credit accounts. Hold your children responsible for their daily lives. Do not pick up after them or do their chores. Allow them to learn by their mistakes. Have them take charge of themselves. Give them guidance, but know where the balance is between guidance and enabling. Let them suffer the consequences of the wrong actions so hopefully they will not repeat the same. When we cover up for them we send the message that, "They are not capable."*

Question 19: Do you recognize any faults in the rehabilitation system? Does health insurance adequately allocate funds towards substance abuse treatment? What costs were incurred by you for the treatment of your son?

Response: *First, and foremost, the problem lies with the fact that information is not readily available. Although the country claims to be educated on the topic of addiction, little information regarding resources is readily available. Even hospitals lack in follow-up procedures. Many medical centers do not offer detoxification and will send a potential overdose case home with little or no intervention. When one is finally admitted for treatment the stay is too short for any substantial progress to occur. The bureaucracy involved for transferring patients from one facility to another is daunting. Often times, parents will relinquish their attempts to admit their child since the system makes it most difficult and frustrating. The "28 Day Rule" for course of treatment is unrealistic and makes it highly unlikely to achieve success. The failure rate for treatment is too often at an increase since at day 28 the user is released. We believe that most of that period is merely an introduction and detoxification effort rather than a behavior modification strategy. More time must be granted for a higher success rate and lower relapse rate. We were fortunate enough to have a facility that was funded by donations and imposed no time constraints on our son's course of treatment. The facility drug tested our son weekly at first and gradually decreased it to a random monthly screening. This was probably helpful in keeping the residents in check. Still there are many cracks in the system, and one such crack is that parents cannot commit their children to treatment if they are unwilling and are over the age of eighteen. So parents are left with their hands tied as their child may continue using, and they have no recourse, consequently resulting in less chance of saving their child.*

The following writings were included in this mother's personal journal which was composed prior to the above interview. A few days after the completion of this interview the "mom" decided to share some of this daily journal. It reflects the feelings she had in reference to her son's chemical dependency. It is emotional, and we did not gain full access to the journal as she provided us with her personal selection of salient points. The following pages express a true introspection of her thoughts.

"I did not realize that you could lose thirty years in just thirty days. It was painful sometimes I had no will to live....I didn't want to die, I just didn't care if I lived...

....There is pre addiction and post addiction. Once you experience addiction in your life there is no going back. I miss the pre addiction life. Wounds are deep yet if you scratch me on the surface I will bleed, it's feeling that fragile....

...Life as you knew it is over....

... Yet there were some positive outcomes from addiction. These include becoming more spiritual, attending peer group meetings, and becoming a stronger person. I even began keeping a journal..."

"In The Wake of The Tsunami- a page from my journal" (1-1-12)

This is how I feel right now. And this is where I am. I am meandering among the wreckage. Picking through the debris of what was. Searching for pieces of the past, scraps of memories, something I can hold onto and treasure. I am wandering through the destruction hoping to find enough to sustain life and carry on...

We knew the tsunami was coming. Back in the fall, the "water" started to recede from the shore, and we knew that something terrible was coming. My husband said to me on several occasions that he had a sense of impending doom. We recognized the signs, we just didn't react quickly enough.

So we did what anyone would do before the monstrous wave hit; we ran. We ran for our lives, tried to outdistance ourselves from the beast' that was bearing down on us. But as hard as we tried, and as fast as we ran, the tsunami' inevitably ripped at our heels, and ultimately swallowed us. Tossing and turning us, churning us around and finally spitting us out. We clung on for dear life... held on in hopes of surviving.

And as the surge of the enormous wave passed, we drew in a deep breath and exhaled with relief.

"We made it !" But the thrill and excitement of having survived was short-lived. As we surveyed the damage around us, we saw what was left in the wake of the tsunami; Slowly accepting this altered landscape as our new reality.

The tsunami has a name, it is called "addiction", and it has claimed my beautiful son. My son doesn't live here anymore. And we now live in the wake of the tsunami;

"My Fears" (1-3-12)

1. I fear that my son will die...from an overdose, or a knife, or a gunshot, or that he will freeze to death out in the street, or a million other horrible ways to die that I imagine.

2. I fear that my son will live...as an addict all the days of his life.

3. I fear that my son will be arrested and go to jail.

4. I fear that my son will never know the happiness of loving someone special, and being loved in return.

5. I fear that my son will be alone, sad, depressed, penniless, and addicted—never realizing his full potential or the vast amount of love that surrounds him.

6. I fear that I will lose my son in my life, and all the hopes and dreams that I had for him.

"Fear and Worry" (1-31-12)

Fear and worry continue to be my biggest enemies. They invade my peace. They haunt my dreams. They make my heart race, my hands shake my stomach churn. I cannot eat. I cannot sleep. I cannot escape these two, worry and fear.

They mock me and my pitiful attempts to 'Let go and let God.' Fear and worry, they know no boundaries. They respect not the hour of day or night. They firmly reside in my heart, soul and mind. They stealthily stalk me, invading the moment between inhale and exhale. They sit on my chest and shake me awake just as I begin to fall asleep. And they are waiting by my side for the instant my eyes open in the morning, to invade my consciousness at first light.

Fear and worry. I have no respite from you. Not a moments rest from you. When things are 'bad', you rage like a wild fire, out of control. When things are 'good', you smolder and burn with a fiery vengeance waiting for your next opportunity to ignite. You are always there, right below the surface, everywhere I go—you go with me.

"It can't happen to me." You think you raise your kids the right way, you go to religion, you do the right things and it still happens. It knows no boundaries. The guilt still falls on the *parents—society believes that the onus rests on the parents when kids violate norms.*

An Interview : The Brother of a Recovering Addict

The following interview was volunteered by an older brother of a recovering drug addict. Throughout the interview the subject will be referred to as "the brother." This interview was prepared to allow the reader to imagine what life is like while living with a chemically dependent person and what life is like while taking the steps towards recovery and rehabilitation.

Question 1: How old are you?

Response: *Twenty-five. I am the older of two children.*

Question 2: What is your occupation?

Response: *I am a middle school Math teacher.*

Question 3: Describe your relationship with your brother prior to his chemical dependency.

Response: *We had a close relationship typical of brothers. We had similar interests. We were interested in sports.*

Question 4: Describe your relationship with your brother as of late.

Response: *Our contact is limited because of rehabilitation restrictions. We are "mending fences."*

Question: 5: Did you sense the usage of drugs during your brother's addiction? What clued you into his addiction?

Response: *After I graduated from high school and entered college, I knew he was smoking pot. I never found any drug paraphernalia except for a marijuana pipe. When he began college, my brother joined a fraternity and had a change of attitude. He refocused his thoughts on lesser issues. My suspicions were realized when I had access to his computer and noticed slang messages with overtones that implicated substance usage. When my brother failed out of his freshman year at college, I saw a message on his computer that read "I went to college for a degree and came out as a drug addict."*

Question 6: Have you ever experimented with drugs? Do you drink alcohol or smoke cigarettes?

Response: *I never experimented with any hard core drugs. I had an occasional drink, and I dipped tobacco. I realized the potential dangers of dipping tobacco and discontinued it.*

Question 7: Did you or any members of your family feel violated by your brother's addiction?

Response: *Feeling violated depended on the circumstances at any given time. I felt sorry for my parents at the beginning, but I saw no fault in their parenting procedures. Over time, I became frustrated because they would not take actions which I thought were appropriate. I saw the necessity to have my brother arrested for criminal*

*activity associated with drugs but my parents
disagreed. I felt stressed when things were not
handled the way I saw fit.*

Question 8: What help, if any, did you seek during
your brother's chemical dependency?

Response: *I never sought help.*

Question 9: What advice would you give others
who have a sibling with a substance abuse problem?

Response: *No bargaining. Set a hard path, be strict,
use a no tolerance approach. There is no reasoning
with the sibling since the craving and drugs to
satisfy it are prevalent in his life. I am happy he is
alive, however, I will always use caution in our
relationship. Remain strong, offer opinions, and
stand tough. Love cannot overcome addiction.
While my brother was under the influence other
people's feelings were not accounted for. The drugs
supersede every personal relationship while the
addict incurs debt.*

Question 10: How were you instrumental in your brother's road to recovery?

Response: *My role was to sometimes serve as a mediator and buffer between my parents and brother. My approach was steadfast allowing for no negotiating, no options—just get help! My brother chose to leave the house at which point he and I had no communication. Eventually, he got help. When my brother accepted rehabilitation, I visited him consistently on a weekly basis. The stress that I felt at times decreased upon subsequent visits as I noticed progress in his treatment. During these visits, I would hug my brother and tell him how proud I was of him and encouraged him to stay strong and keep up the good work. The visits have been reduced as I try to balance my professional and personal schedule.*

Question 11: Do you believe that the system provided adequate care for your brother?

Response: *Thus far I am impressed with the rehabilitation system, but remain concerned with the amount of freedom for a recovering addict. This freedom allows my brother to leave the facility and it scares me but I know it's necessary as part of the treatment for him to rehabilitate and be a part of the socialization process. The discharge of my brother from the facility will bring upon additional stresses and concerns as rehabilitation is a whole new process to contend with.*

Interviews with Police Officers

The following interviews were granted to us by two police officers from an area in the United States which is populated with a mixed culture and is plagued with a heavy incidence of substance abuse and solicitation. The officers provided information associated with arrests related to drug possession and gave some insight as to how the problem is escalating in select parts of this particular area. Bear in mind that the officers, although employed by a large law enforcement agency, along with fellow officers, play an integral role in the apprehension and prosecution of criminals. The information forthcoming is a matter of public record and is only a small indication of the magnitude of the problem. Each officer was interviewed independent of each other but were asked the same questions. We will refer to them as "Officer 1" and "Officer 2".

Question 1: How long have you been a police officer?

Response:

Officer 1-- *Twenty-two years*

Officer 2—*Thirty-three years*

Question 2: What is your current role?

Response:

Officer 1-- *I enforce laws and apprehend criminals.*

Officer 2-- *I am a retired detective from a large suburban police agency.*

Question 3: As a police officer, what, in your opinion, is the percentage of substance abusers you arrest in a given year amongst all your arrests?

Response:

Officer 1-- *About 70% of people I encounter who defy the law are using drugs. They are either using one drug or combining substances. A search warrant is sometimes obtained based on probable cause, or in some instances, reasonable suspicion of possession, sale and use of drugs. If drugs are discovered on the person who is being arrested, no warrant is necessary to further charge the person for the possession of drugs.*

Officer 2-- *A vast majority of arrests were drug-related. If those I arrested weren't actually using drugs, they were often found to be affiliated in some way, even remotely, with the drug community. Many of those arrested are living in areas where drug use and sales are rampant.*

Question 4: What would you say is the most frequently abused substances used by the people you arrest?

Response:

Officer 1-- *The two most frequent drugs used amongst those arrested are oxycodone and heroin. Derivatives of opiates (pain medications) are the most sought after drugs.*

Officer 2-- *During my tenure, crack/cocaine were the most prevalent. That has changed, although these drugs are still widely used. However, whenever one drug trend decreases a new one emerges, such as the current trend in usage of pain pills and heroin. As usual, the current trend only remains as such until another one prevails. With many of these drugs such as crack, it starts as a one-time experiment and becomes a lifetime addiction.*

Question 5:   Once a substance user is in custody, how often, if ever, has he or she asked for your help in getting clean?

 Response:

Officer 1-- *The users are in and out of rehabilitation and are generally not interested in police intervention for help. We arrest them, and they usually cooperate so that they may be processed accordingly and hopefully move on in the quest to get high again.*

Officer 2-- *In my career several individuals have asked for help to get clean after the arrest and booking. If I saw redeeming qualities in a person, I would initiate dialogue regarding my assisting in seeking rehabilitative services and options. The job of a police officer goes beyond the realm of arrest.*

Officers can offer a myriad of agencies and are good resources for an offender to look to in order to get back on a functional path in society.

Question 6: Explain the process of drug court.

Response:

Officer 1-- *The accused is brought into the precinct upon arrest. After processing at the precinct the person is arraigned and bail may not always be granted. The previous record of the accused is taken into account before bail is set. If the record is extensive, then bail may be denied. The officer who made the arrest is asked to testify at the time of trial. The other alternative, provided there is an underlying or blatant addiction, is drug court. Drug treatment court is an alternative to incarceration for drug abusing defendants. Drug court provides programs for those who plead guilty to the charges applied to them and who are eligible for the program. If the offender refuses drug court as an alternative, he or she will be processed according to conventional criminal justice protocol.*

Officer 2-- *One may be eligible for drug court if the offense warrants this procedure. Felony-level drug sale offenders are not permitted in drug court, as the most severe A-1 and A-2 drug felony offenders are also precluded from this venue. If eligible, the offender is ordered to treatment facilities involving education, treatment, and case management. This is sometimes a proactive approach in the handling of drug offenses, yet can fail if the offender does not adhere to specifications outlined through the drug court. Violation of drug court procedures can remand participants to prison. Participants are assigned a case manager who will monitor the progress of the individual who must appear periodically before a drug court judge to discuss and document his or her progress. Case managers accompany the participants when in court.*

Question 7: Do you recognize any faults in the law enforcement/legal system with respect to chemical dependency? Do you think punishment is fitting in most arrests?

Response:

Officer 1-- *Since the society treats drug addiction as an illness, the consequences are often not what some might believe is appropriate. The users know how to "play" the system and may be granted less of a punishment. If the addict becomes an informant, and cases are discovered and found to be substantial, the courts may provide leniency in punishment. Rehabilitation does not work for everyone who enters and therefore is not always the most effective way to separate users from the rest of society. In many cases, the rehabilitation process does not provide ample sanctions for the use and sale of illegal substances, therefore more needs to be addressed in the legal and rehabilitative systems with respect to policy.*

Officer 2-- *Decent people who are chemically dependent do not usually look to harm others, yet will go to some lengths to replenish their habit. The system places the proper sanction for any given crime including drug sales, possession and use. I never met a "junkie" who was happy living a life as a user. The justice system often places these people in the appropriate venue for evaluation, trial, and treatment. The offenders know how to "play" the system in an attempt to avoid harsher punishment.*

Question 8: Please provide your encounters with processing and apprehending those associated with drug crimes.

Response:

Officer 1-- *Once the drug user or dealer is located, an arrest is made, and he is brought into the police precinct where he is processed, possibly finger-printed, and then awaits arraignment. Most of the offenders adhere to procedures without incidence or resistance, yet some are violent.*

Officer 2-- *Upon arrest, drug perpetrators often remain "tame," meek, or calm. This will depend on the substance that has been ingested. If the drug taken causes lethargy, then the arrest is usually uneventful with little opposition. Conversely, if the drug has stimulating effects, it may cause resistance on the part of the user upon arrest. This may cause confrontation, but is not necessarily the norm in most arrests of this nature. Cooperation can facilitate the process for hopefully a favorable outcome.*

Question 9: Do users generally partake in distribution of the illegal substances?

Response:

Officer 1-- *A large population of the users solicit for the sake of maintaining their own habit. Some distribute for large monetary gain, but most sell to keep the supply readily available for their own use.*

Officer 2-- *Not always. Some users distribute their supply to others not for monetary reasons, but simply to hide their stock.*

Question 10: Do the offenders "rat" on others who are using and distributing drugs when they are apprehended?

Response:

Officer 1-- *Users will often inform law enforcement of activity they are aware of. This happens when they are at odds with another dealer or are looking for revenge. Leniency in punishment is also a motivation for a person to inform law enforcement officials.*

Officer 2-- *Everybody "rats!" Given the right*

circumstances, drug offenders are reliable informants. This community knows no loyalty. It is all about survival of self.

Question 11: What is the average age among those arrested for use and sale of illegal substances?

Response:

Officer 1-- *The average ages are from 18-29. Some users are younger while others are older, but most fall into this age range.*

Officer 2-- *Average age of users ranged from 18-40. However, bear in mind that many users fall below and above this age range.*

An Interview With An Addiction Specialist

The next interview was conducted with the cooperation of an addiction counselor whose expertise gave insight to the magnitude of the chemical dependency problem in society. Throughout her career, she has seen many people who were plagued by chemical dependency. Some of the users are worse than others, yet the commonality is that they all show signs of addiction. In addition, all treatment plans are devised according to the individual and his or her particular addiction.

Question 1: What is your role in substance abuse treatment?

Response: *I am a Prevention Coordinator in Addiction Recovery Services for an area facility.*

Question 2: As an addiction counselor, what do you see as the most widely used drug of late?

Response: *Among youth, alcohol and marijuana are prevalent. This is followed by prescription drugs and heroin.*

Question 3: What age groups are most prevalent in seeking treatment for addiction?

Response: *The ages that I most frequently encounter for treatment range from 25-45 years old.*

Question 4: How successful, overall, is treatment today as compared to a decade ago?

Response: *Treatment is more sophisticated today. However, treatment is only as successful as we make it. More is offered in the way of treatment. There is more recognition of concurrent disorders. For example, we cite the incidence of depression and usage and have an understanding of the relationship between the two. Treatment is mandated today by the criminal justice system. This is an improvement, since we are realizing that treatment can be more beneficial than incarceration alone for the crime. In this decade, family has become more of an integral part of the treatment process. This is an advancement in treatment, as the family is a key to recovery. Therefore, the system offers peripheral services to include family intervention and rehabilitation of the user.*

Question 5: Do you recognize shortcomings of the healthcare system with respect to substance abuse?

Response: *There are some problems that need to be addressed. The system needs to recognize chemical dependency as a disease, thereby instituting policies that use the medical model to dictate treatment. The society has long seen the addict as a criminal and delayed or even avoided using funds to treat the problem as an illness. Shifting the focus from crime to disease will be a process—one worth enduring. Drug abuse is a chronic progressive disease and has commanded a lot of out-of-pocket expense. Other illnesses require a co-pay at the time of a visit to a provider, yet drug-related visits are not always covered in the manner that conventional illnesses are.*

Question 6: Have you experienced any personal affliction with substance abuse? How did you become involved in this career?

Response: *When I was nine years old, I went to an AA meeting with my uncle. He was an alcoholic going through recovery. Addictive personalities tend to run in families. My brother succumbed to chemical dependency which also gave me the impetus to pursue this career. In addition, my mother went through emotional difficulties which may have fueled my interest in this field.*

Question 7: What do you see as a future in this country with respect to addiction?

Response: *As this problem evolves, more high-end drugs may surface. As pharmaceutical companies research and market drugs, they will swiftly move through society as doctors prescribe medication for many ailments. The face of the addict may change. The legalization of once illegal substances may create a new generation of users. As of this writing, the recent legalization of marijuana in two states in America, in my opinion, compromises the ability to prevent further, more dangerous use of drugs. Since anyone can become an addict, with the advent of new drugs, we are vulnerable to new experimentation.*

Question 8: What, in your professional opinion, is the "gateway" drug to more complex substances?

Response: *Alcohol and marijuana are usually the first drugs associated with the term "gateway."*

Question 9: What combinations of drugs are most commonly experimented with?

Response: *Alcohol combined with any other drug is typically a recipe for the users.*

Question 10: What are the most significant reasons for the beginning of habitual drug use?

Response: *The number one reason why teens begin using drugs is peer pressure. Low self- esteem increases the fear of not fitting in with the group, thereby, raising the chances of experimentation. To belong to the group, one will often fall prey to the risky behaviors in which the group is involved. Depression is being diagnosed more so today than in past decades. Depression is a "catch-22" since it can be caused by a number of factors which lead to drug use, and is sometimes treated with medication that has a strong potential for dependency. In the case of individuals diagnosed with ADHD (Attention Deficit Hyperactivity Disorder) the risk of dependency is noted to be higher. The policies for treatment of ADHD have often been criticized as too liberal as the use of Adderall has skyrocketed among students. While a course of drug treatment for this disorder has proven effective, others have obtained these drugs for the sole purpose of recreational use. In addition, students without the disorder rely on these drugs for increased concentration and enhanced academic performance. In actuality, Adderall and Ritalin, two widely prescribed drugs, are used to improve concentration in the ADHD patient. However, when taken without medical supervision, they may cause adverse effects. The reactions can be dangerous and even fatal, as with any drug taken out of context. People go through lifestyle changes. These changes sometimes bring about the use of drugs when adapting to these changes becomes difficult.*

Question 11:   What is the role of parents and family in prevention and recovery?

Response: Boundaries need to be set and consequences for deviant behavior must be imposed. It is the primary responsibility of the parents or guardian to outline rules which pertain to the children from early on. These rules must be sanctioned immediately if violated.

These interviews brought upon many emotions between the interviewers and interviewees. We hope that the reader has gained a sense of the strife that many go through because of chemical dependency and how it influences all institutions in society.

Anyone who has attended one of my assemblies knows the ground rules. We treat each other with respect, we keep our cell phones and our devices in the "off" position. If an emergency arises, you are advised to excuse yourself from the program and tend to the matter. Additionally, I have built-in breaks in my programs, wherein my audience gets to stand, stretch their legs, talk to friends, and refocus. When I resume the assembly, I once again appreciate your undivided attention. This is the point in my book where I invite you to take such a break. Thank you for your attention thus far.

Welcome Back

Chapter 6

The Big Black Book

"Athletes, artists, all-around good people, historic figures, teachers, and professionals all adorned this book."

In November of 1986, I was assigned to the recruitment section of the Suffolk County Police Department. Herein my duties included visiting high schools, colleges, community organizations, and addressing audiences on how to educationally and socially prepare themselves for a possible career in law enforcement. My lectures included dialogue for testing procedures, written examinations, the interview process, medical examinations, physical agility tests, psychological examinations, polygraph, and applicants' background investigation. Additionally, I would discuss police academy training and opportunities for advancement and transfer within the police department. In the many years I spent in the recruitment section, I was fortunate to meet many exemplary human beings of all ages.

In 1995, I decided to memorialize these individuals by taking their autographs and photos, placing them in an album, and with their permission or that of a family member, telling their stories. The individuals whose autographs I collected were those of scholar athletes, academic achievers, the artistically inclined, the physically challenged, reformed bullies, military heroes, survivors of accident, illness or tragedy, and those who perished in past years. Also included are celebrities from all walks of life and well-regarded and respected members of society. The book contains a picture and story of whom, in my opinion, was the greatest man who lived, namely my father, Paul Failla. As you see, I carry my father's name and do so with honor and pride.

Regrettably, I cannot mention all of the names in the *Black Book* since there are too many to count. It does not lessen the effect these people have had in my life or what they have contributed to society. I carry the *Book* to all of my speaking engagements and refer to the many people in it who enrich our lives. As I encounter so many different personalities among my audiences, I ask some of my participants to sign a card and I place it in my *Book* with a special story about the person. I have cherished these stories and the people connected to them and I refer to them throughout my programs. These remarkable people share so many admirable character traits. These include leadership, courage, fortitude, respect, accountability for their actions, and intelligence. In addition, they all leave an indelible mark on society. Their accomplishments are monumental and teach us the values so instrumental in living productive lives. The people have been through tragedy, turmoil, strife, success, and happiness. However, regardless of what they endured, they persevered and thrived. These inspiring stories will forever remain an integral part of my message.

Sharing some of the memories helps to inspire and motivate audiences. Therefore, I would like to include some highlights of my *Black Book* with my readers. College and high school athletes have been a salient part of my programs since they overcome many adversities and endure tremendous competition to succeed. Jack was a thirteen year-old middle school student, who I met through his mother, an alumni of my high school. Jack was a respectful young man with a tremendous talent for bowling. He rolled his first perfect game (a score of 300) at the age of eight. As of February 2011, Jack has rolled eighteen perfect games and six "800" series. Jack was also second in the country with a 220.54 college bowling average. We have maintained a friendship, and I am proud to have him as a friend. Jami, a young woman, and point-after kicker on the boys' varsity football team in high school appeared in a Super Bowl ad extolling the accomplishments of several high school football players throughout the country. Jami went on to play soccer at a Division I private university in New York. Honorio and Joel, both New York Daily News Golden Gloves boxers, were top flight contenders in the competition. Kerry, a New York State high school wrestling champion and national collegiate champion was a two-time Olympian in the free style heavy weight wrestling ranks. He joins Jesse, a six-time Suffolk County wrestling champion, four-time New York State champion in high school, and an all-American and National Champion on the Ivy League collegiate level. Both exude the desire, diligence, and work ethic it takes to be a winner. Kristen, a member of her high school cheerleading squad, was part of a contingent that cheered at the NFL Pro Bowl during her senior year of high school. She is a dedicated athlete who participated on a college squad and became a professional cheerleader for an NFL franchise. Justin, a high school football player and a young man of impressive stature, went on to play   college football at his Ivy League school as an offensive lineman. Rick, a high school baseball player with a 93mph fastball was a first team all-American who rated as the number 1 player in New York State. Rick was drafted by a major league franchise and played in the minor leagues. These outstanding athletes shared the motivation to achieve and the qualities so deemed in the quintessential scholar athlete.

Despite adversity, these next role models overcame it and soared to heights unbeknownst to them. Scott, afflicted with cerebral palsy, graduated with a Bachelor's Degree in Technology Studies from the New York State University system and dedicates much of his time advocating for the physically challenged. Antonio, a blind young man, was a high school student who played the drums, saxophone, piano, and guitar. He was also a member of his high school and church concert bands. Antonio went on to become a student at a local community college. Brooke was eleven years old and while walking home on her first day of seventh grade, she was struck by a car. This accident nearly took her life and left her in a quadriplegic state. This beautiful, intelligent, and sensitive young girl regained her ability to speak and retained her desire to fulfill her goals. Although her goals may have shifted due to the tragic event, she maintained focus, finished school, and attended Harvard University. Upon graduation, she delivered a heartwarming address to the graduating class and penned a book along with her mom on her story. She continued at Harvard University for graduate level study, earned her Master's Degree and recently earned her Doctorate Degree from Stony Brook University. Brooke has made numerous public appearances and is an advocate of the physically challenged. In addition, she teaches and has served on many government committees. Brooke brings a message of hope, inspiration, and kindness throughout the country.

This next category I reference involves serious or fatal automobile crashes. Michael's story is one I portray in detail during my Driver Safety Awareness Program. Michael was a young man who resided in my neighborhood and lost his life one evening when his car unexpectedly left the roadway and struck a tree. His untimely death affected many people. Michael was a personable young man who enjoyed life as a high school athlete with many friends and came from a model family. Colin, a high school senior, approached me after an assembly I conducted for his senior class and inquired about becoming a police officer. Approximately one month later, Colin lost his life in a motor vehicle accident where he was a passenger in his friend's car en route to a mall to shop for prom tuxedos. Both Michael's and Colin's fathers passed away seven years after the tragic loss of their sons. I guess the warranty on a broken heart is seven years. I was approached by a college student who emotionally recounted the passing of his sixteen year-old cousin who was killed in a motor vehicle accident in Pennsylvania several days prior to that classroom visit. I mention this briefly in chapter 3. His cousin, Casey, was one of five teenagers who all perished in the accident. Her funeral was postponed while awaiting family to arrive from Europe. Upon returning from his cousin's funeral, the student presented me with Casey's funeral prayer card and reiterated the following story. A member of the clergy from Casey's parish was visiting Rome at the time of the accident and was granted an audience with the Pope. The Pope was moved by this tragic story and included the names of the five victims in one of his sermons. It just goes to show the far-reaching effect tragedies such as this have on everyone. Doug was a high school classmate of mine who made me realize that I was mortal. Doug was a scholar-athlete who possessed an altruistic personality with a kind word for everyone he knew. Two years after high school, Doug was driving home from an upstate university where he was a student and lost his life in a car crash. At his wake, I remember thinking, as I looked around, that anyone in attendance could easily meet the same fate as Doug. I also remember thinking at twenty years old that if my friends and I live to be forty, Doug would be gone twenty years. Well, many of us have passed that age, and I think now of what Doug was denied because of his shortened life.   Adam, a senior in high school, approached me after a presentation and relayed the following story. Several years before our meeting, he was struck by a car and his family was told he would never walk again. Adam went on to become the captain of his high school track team and a marathon runner. Nicholas, a high school student, was fortunate to have a good Samaritan summon help when he fell off of his bicycle and collided with the windshield of a parked vehicle, cutting open his jugular vein. He told me he was on the brink of death when his heart stopped beating and his breathing ceased. Listening to him telling this story made me realize that I couldn't imagine the world without his presence. While some stories bring sadness, I am honored to uphold memories of these notable young people and their accomplishments to motivate others to live life to the fullest.

I was fortunate enough to meet and take a photograph with, or obtain an autograph from, many celebrities. They included recording artists Billy Joel, Frankie Valli, Constantine Maroulis, and Peter Yarrow. Star athletes include Pete Rose, Goose Gossage, Art Shamsky, Vijay Singh, George Chuvalo, Lisa Fernandez, Stephon Marbury, Sebastian Telfair, Maria Michta , Henrik Lundqvist, Sue Bird, and Amos Zereoue. Actress, Jamie Lynn Sigler, appears in the pages of *The Black Book.* Breanne Stark, a ballet dancer, graces my book as well.

A representation of the military in the *Black Book* makes me most proud. Jeans Cruz was among one of the American soldiers who bravely spotted Saddam Hussein in a small bunker and assisted in capturing the dictator of Iraq. Michael Murphy was a United States Navy Seal who realized his lifelong goal to become a Navy Seal and gave his life for the freedom of the people of the world. The sister of SPC Orlando A. Perez was so proud of her brother who was killed in action in Operation Iraqi Freedom, that she respectfully requested her brother's name and picture be displayed in the *Book.* I was honored and proud to do so. World War II veteran, Bernie Rader, was a wounded POW and part of the only exchange between Allied Forces and the Germans. He was classified as a war hero. Andrew Burian, Holocaust survivor, appears in the *Book,* and we met in a school where he was delivering an account of his experience. I met the nephew of veteran David Thomas Montgomery who passed on January 15, 2008. Montgomery, a World War II United States Navy radioman, orated the infamous first message of the attack on Pearl Harbor, December 7, 1941 when he stated, "AIR RAID, PEARL HARBOR, THIS IS NO DRILL." A student asked that his father, a United States soldier who was stationed in Kuwait, be honored in the book for which I graciously complied.

I took the autographs of two high school basketball stars on the same day. One year later, one was gunned down and lost his life in an altercation provoked by another party at a gas station. Two years after I received their autographs, the second basketball player was the shooting victim in a highly controversial racial profiling incident. Thankfully, this victim survived. Next, an aspiring athlete whose life was cut short at fourteen years old was the tragic victim of drowning due to a capsized boat. He has a place in the *Book*. A young man named Kevin, a freshman at his high school where I was conducting an assembly for his entire grade level, asked me if he could take the microphone and speak to his peers for a moment. This young man captured the attention of over three hundred young adults when he spoke about the pain that a victim of ridicule endures. He was one such victim and used his circumstance to relay anti-bullying and anti-ridicule messages. Upon conclusion of his talk, this young man received a resounding ovation from his classmates. Undoubtedly, this student changed perception and received much praise and high accolades from his peers that day. Additionally, his high school recognized him for this unsolicited message and honored him with an exceptional student award which he received at an open Board of Education meeting.

These final two stories regarding inductees to *The Book* reference September 11, 2001, a sad day in the history of the world. I recently met a wonderful couple, John and Jan Vigiano, whose family was torn apart by the events that day. Their sons, John, a

New York City firefighter, who followed in his father's career footsteps, and Joseph, a New York City emergency service detective, both lost their lives as a result of this attack on our nation. These two men rendered the ultimate sacrifice, their lives, by attempting to save victims of this tragedy. Both men answered their calling. While the masses were attempting to escape, these brave men and their colleagues were going forward to save lives. They are true heroes.

While preparing to begin an assembly at a Long Island high school, four young male students entered and quickly sat themselves in the back of the room. I summoned them to the front, gave them each a nickname and included them in a role-play portion of my program. Upon conclusion of the assembly, one of these young men remained behind to speak with me. His name was Josh Stone, who I nicknamed as "Scooter." Josh reiterated a question that I pose when I am speaking—"When was the last time you told your dad ,'I love you'?" I told Josh that I ask this question in every assembly I conduct. I went on to ask him, "Can you remember?" He stated, "Not really," and I was thinking go home tonight and just say it. He then said, "I think it was very late at night on September 10th or very early in the morning on September 11th ,2001." He advised me that on the morning of September 11th his father (Lonny Stone) caught the 6:59 am Long Island Railroad train from Bellmore to Penn Station. He got to his office at 8:15 am. He stated, "My father's office was on the 92nd floor of Twin Tower # 1. At 8:46 am the first jet crashed into the 94th floor of Twin Tower # 1, and I never saw my father again. I was eight years old when this happened, and it really bothers me that I can't remember the last time I told my dad 'I love you'." Saddened, I was able to extend my condolences and offered an apology if my program set off painful emotions. That afternoon while attending my daughter's field hockey game, I received a call from Josh's mother, Stacey Stone, who wanted to thank me for the words I spoke in the assembly. She told me that since Josh participated in my assembly he was able to express his inner most feelings about the loss of his father. Stacey and I arranged a meeting with Josh and over the years our families have become friends. I believe Josh said it all in the following excerpts from his college admissions essay:

"My freshmen year in high school I met a man who I would have never thought would have such an impact on my life and my maturity, Retired Suffolk County Police Officer, Paul Failla. Every year Paul Failla tells my story to the new freshman class.... I have become a symbol of how loss doesn't define you, but it shapes you. What I've learned from this is now an understanding; I must be more true to myself without care of others' judgments, freedom to grieve the loss of my dad, and a new appreciation for improving myself so I can reach my full potential. I am hopeful that my experiences at college will help me in becoming an even more responsible and wise young adult.....I know how important the upcoming years are and I plan to work meticulously to do what is needed for me to make my college experience worthwhile."

From the day I met Josh till he graduated, he received permission to attend subsequent assemblies I performed at his high school where I retold the story of his father, Lonny, and our meeting. The Stone family has given me permission to include this story as a permanent part of my character education program.

So whether celebrity or not, these people have possessed the desire to accomplish goals and the motivation to succeed. Goal-oriented personality traits are those that last a lifetime and define who we are. They are the legacy we engrave in our epitaphs.

Chapter 7

Rites of Passage

"Congratulations! You made it."

Rites of passage are the ceremonies associated with the moving from one life phase to another significant one. With each passage, we are continually proving to ourselves and others that we are mature, responsible, and intelligent enough while striving to attain our ultimate goals. When the goals of one milestone are met the pursuit is to meet another. Examples of rites of passages include graduations, obtaining a driver's license, marriage, religious ceremonies, coming of age for certain privileges, beginning college, and becoming a parent. While there are many rites of passage, some events associated with these are addressed in detail in my programs. I discuss driving, graduations, high school proms, and college; all of which often come within a one-year time span. The great majority of young adults relish these times and fare well, while others have faltered and made destructive choices thereby having negative consequences. These consequences could possibly linger indefinitely. Many times, peer pressure plays a significant role in the choices we make in these situations. Sometimes in an attempt to fit in, we place ourselves in compromising positions. Although the "Uh Oh Switch" went off inside of us, we put common sense aside and go forth anyway. Once we make this choice, we have to be prepared to handle anything good, bad, or indifferent that may come our way. Be ever mindful of who and what is affected by our choices.

In the case of proms, the rules of etiquette are clearly defined by the school administration prior to the event. Often times, students are required to attend a pre-prom seminar with their parents and their dates. Pre-prom responsibilities lie with the students and their parents. Responsibility at the event lies with the school district, its administrators, chaperones, and the students. In school districts where a code of conduct exists, this policy is strictly enforced, whether the prom takes place on or off the school property. After-prom plans not sponsored by the school district are, once again, the responsibility of the parents and students. Be aware that one's conduct during any phase of the prom experience is a direct reflection on the student's living and learning community. Many schools currently host proms in close proximity to graduation. This methodology serves a purpose; first it requires the students to remain within close distance of their homes, thereby eliminating out of state overnight concerns; second it minimizes the occurrence of accidents which result from destructive decision-making that may often result in injury or fatality. Although some of these events are supervised, there can be incidences which ultimately spill over to affect the graduation of a student or students. The severity of a destructive decision will determine the consequences. The most severe consequence of wrongful behavior at a prom is being denied the opportunity to walk at graduation and to receive your diploma with the rest of the graduating class. People have been turned away for scholarships or entrance into colleges or the military and prosecuted because of abusing or misunderstanding this rite of passage.

Some schools reward students entering their senior year of high school with the privilege of leaving school premises during lunch hours. This open campus policy has unfortunately proven to be troublesome and tragic in some cases. It is problematic since often students do not return to campus on time or choose not to return at all. Many students speed through neighborhood streets to try and beat the time constraints. This has led to tragedy in several instances in which students, other motorists, and passengers were involved in fatal motor vehicle crashes. It is not an accepted excuse for lateness to claim that traffic, lines in a food establishment or convenience store, prevented one from entering the school building promptly. Some schools have been proactive in amending the policy to allow students to leave the premises during lunch periods only if weather permits. Some schools offer an alternative to open campus by providing a senior lounge or cafeteria which exclusively admits seniors. This has resulted in curtailed problematic activity, yet some schools still maintain open campus procedures no matter what the weather conditions are. In any case, the policies are enforced by each individual school district whose administrators outline the given procedures. This policy requires strict security measures insuring that underclassmen not entitled to this privilege do not leave school grounds during any lunch period. As a parent, I was not an advocate of the open campus policy. I felt more at ease knowing that my child did not leave school until dismissal time at the end of the day. Even though this policy is enacted by the school, the parent has the final word when granting permission for the child to leave the building during school hours. If the parent refuses to sign the permission form, the student will not be allowed to exit the school. However, the possibility of leaving exists since some students elect to depart during lunch periods in an unauthorized fashion.

Another privilege granted by high schools is on-campus parking for legally licensed students. This privilege comes with written guidelines that must be strictly adhered to by the students. To reinforce these guidelines, many schools adapt an awareness program for the student and their parents. Mandating parental attendance does not insinuate wrong doing or lack of knowledge, but is quality time spent with their child while educating, re-educating and reiterating what they already have imparted in their sons and daughters. Attendance at these workshops gains eligibility for the student to park their vehicle on school grounds in designated student parking areas. Inadequate academic performance, disciplinary issues, and infraction of vehicle and traffic laws may cause this privilege to be rescinded.

High school years bring on many celebrations among friends and peers. One such celebration is the Sweet 16 party, marking the milestone birthday of a young woman. The hosts of these parties know who they are going to invite. Discretion in this area is the better part of valor. Distributing invitations at school has been largely replaced by the posting of such an event on social network websites. While this brings extreme joy and the feeling of inclusion for the invited guests, exclusion brings far more pain than many anticipate. I view exclusion as a form of bullying. The host may not intentionally want to cause hurt to her excluded guests, but ultimately does so when she makes her party public amongst all of her peers. The logical way to avoid the feelings of exclusion by others is to use the "snail mail system" and send the invitations directly to the recipients' homes. The Sweet 16 party can spiral out of control if unsupervised. Often, teenagers believe that they are adult enough to engage in behavior that may be harmful or unlawful, for instance drinking alcohol. Therefore, it is important for parents, party-goers, and parents of guests to work cooperatively to curtail or eliminate any risky behaviors.

One major milestone in a teen's life is the approval

to carry a credit card. With this rite of passage comes a monumental responsibility and the evaluation of spending patterns. The credit card companies are interested in obtaining customers and have in some cases been remiss in addressing the spending trends in young first-time cardholders. Recently, credit card reform bills have amended the rules for all cardholders in order to protect the consumer against fraud, identity theft, and undue spending. The outward abuse of credit card expense has become a nationwide problem that called for government intervention in distribution of cards and the limitations on them. One such enacted legislation requires that a person under the age of 21 have a cosigner on the credit card account and that the credit card limit of expenditures must be approved by the adult cosigner, who also approves an increase of credit line. Time constraints occur on all notifications regarding credit cards and policies attached to them, such as increases or decreases in interest rates, yearly cardholder fees and the like. Billing cycles are clearly defined and must be disclosed upon release of the card to the consumer. The notification of such policies, if adhered to, serves to control problems with cardholders somewhat, but if the cardholder fails to read and interpret the guidelines for owning the card, breach of usage may occur. This leads to mistakes in spending and unnecessary or frivolous spending, which in turn may cause a person to incur debt and ultimately raise the possibility of unacceptable credit scores. In turn, when the time comes for a mortgage application or personal loan, it is denied. The country has seen an upswing in credit card use and a downturn in cash spending. Young first time users need to be aware of the disadvantages of credit cards and at the same time be mindful of the independence the cards provide.

Going to college is one of the major milestones in one's life. While it is certainly a *privilege* to attend college, students in today's world are *expected* to attend since the economy commands at least a two year, but preferably a four or more year college education in order for a young adult to be marketable. College years begin at approximately 18 years of age and are combined with the feeling of being an independent adult and taking on a new role. Many new responsibilities occur as a college student; some students are up to the task, while others find it difficult to immerse themselves in this newly prescribed role. The young adult now has to create a balance between social activities and school obligations. Issues arise when this balance is upset by one outweighing the other. Students who attend as scholarship recipients for sports, arts, or academics have an added responsibility to perform up to the standards as prescribed by each scholarship. As students approach their junior year of college, they often choose to live off campus, work, and own a vehicle. This combination is not always as easy as it sounds. Academic requirements become more difficult and social life may have to subside. This "conflict," if not resolved, will ultimately lead to academic failure, possible probation, or academic dismissal, thereby damaging career aspirations. The development of social, emotional, and intellectual activity during the time between age 18 and 21 is still quite active, thus making it a challenge for some young adults to make the most rational decisions. Another opportunity is the invitation to affiliate with a fraternity or sorority. Some of these are sanctioned, others are not. However, all require the act of pledging to earn passage into these organizations. Acts of pledging are sometimes unacceptable, destructive, or deceiving, while others propel community service, campus responsibility, and unity among schoolmates. One should not subject himself or herself to harm and might find it hard to resist since belonging and acceptance are clear objectives of fraternities and sororities.

Be conscious of hazing, its effects, and the devastation it has on its victims. Unfortunately, some fraternal organizations require acts of hazing for initiation. Stay away from these and find campus sanctioned organizations. Some students find it necessary to work or complete an internship related to their program of study. This provides an even more restricted amount of time in the students' schedule and causes some to feel overwhelmed. It is said that many people meet their future spouses through college. This is a time for exploring serious relationships and may be another obstacle for those who cannot find balance amongst all the aspects of this life stage. Although these relationships are typically supposed to create happiness, they can lead to despair. Learning how to cope with the bumps in relationships will pull you through even the most difficult times. When students leave high school to attend college, they may depart from the ones they dated during those years and attempt a long distance relationship. Sometimes it works and other times it fails. The distance between two people can bring tension and be a distraction. It is not always destined for failure, but one should not underestimate the effects of the long distance relationship on college performance. It is highly recommended that students do not make their decisions to attend a college based on high school relationships, but to choose the college on its reputation and academic strengths. Colleges provide counseling centers in which students can visit trained personnel for guidance on any issues that arise in their college lives, whether personal, professional, or academic. Choose the college with a positive attitude and the willingness to meet a wide variety of personalities. Either way, it is a new venture and should be thoroughly embraced.

Other relationships include friendships. College friends are those who will be connected to you for much of your adult life. Roommates are amongst the first connection of college friends, although the roommate relationship is sometimes overplayed, meaning that so much is invested in this. The selection process has become more intricate as one looks for certain criteria in a roommate. Yet as questionnaires attempt to create the "perfect match," roommates can drift apart and move on to others. That is fine as long as compromise is maintained. Roommates need to adjust to each others' habits and realize that a situation can always be modified if need be. Ideally, we want to get along with our roommates, but in reality, that is not always the case. College students should aim for their goals in friendships, academics, and careers. Hopefully, upon graduation, they will be prepared to enter a competitive job market as a responsible candidate, while the lessons imparted by parents, guardians, and educators maintain a positive impact.

Chapter 8

Ethics

"Our moral programming guides us through life's choices. The programming may stay constant, yet the situations we face are forever changing."

How does one know when he is faced with an ethical dilemma? The answer is obvious. If we feel tension when faced with a compromising situation, we recognize the ethical dilemma. The mere recognition of feeling compromised is, in fact, a sign of a healthy, well-programmed moral character. Humans are dealt ethical scenarios on a daily basis. It is a fairly routine part of our existence, but reconciling the issues is not so simple. Countless scholars, philosophers, and behaviorists have attempted to examine ethics. However, no one yet has been able to clearly define right from wrong in many of the situations we are confronted with. There are guidelines provided to help us select the most ethical choices and still we falter in our decisions concerning ethical dilemmas.

Each of us is committed to a scale of values. Our values are what define us as people. In order to understand our ethical process, we must first realize where our value system originates and how it is maintained throughout our lives. Values are defined as what society deems as good, right, and desirable. Values lay the foundation for how we live our lives. One's value system is instilled in us by our initial educators in life which include parents and guardians. Family is recognized as the most important agent of socializing us into a value system. Subsequent educators such as teachers, clergy, and guidance personnel reinforce our value system. Along with the aforementioned, peer groups, work environment, mass media, and community are instrumental in developing and maintaining our values. When confronted with an ethical situation a person must ask himself, "What is the right thing to do and how will this reflect my value system?" A good decision will enhance your values, whereas a bad decision could have the potential of destroying your life. Following are cases in which one's moral character is put to the test:

Case 1

An act as simple as receiving the wrong change for a purchase we make presents an ethical course of action.

The proper course of action is to alert the cashier of the mistake. If you are overcompensated, then it is your ethical responsibility to return the money; if you are shortchanged, then you are morally obligated to collect the proper change. For if you do not take the moral high road, the onus falls on the cashier to explain the difference to management at the end of his or her shift. Ultimately, the possibly exists that the cashier is obliged to reimburse the business. This author would acknowledge the error and alert the cashier of the mistake.

What would you do?

Case 2

Several years ago, I received a telephone call from a friend requesting my advice. His son found a bag containing approximately $1,100.00 in cash. He was walking through a wooded area, when he kicked a log and noticed a small shopping bag. Naturally, curiosity caused him to open the bag, and he discovered the cash. My friend asked me what *course of action should be taken to rectify the problem.*

Irrespective of where the money came from, I advised him that there was only one acceptable course of action. In this case, one might speculate as to where the source of the money was generated. However, that is not a factor in the end result. This author would escort his son to the local police precinct, file a report claiming found property, have the officer invoice the cash to the property bureau, retain a copy of the report number and the inventory receipt. Be advised that there is no monetary value required as a minimum when submitting found property to the police. Bear in mind, the old adage "finders, keepers, losers, weepers" should not carry influence on the decision to surrender the property. The police department will secure this property for a period of time and if unclaimed, your son would be entitled to collect it. If claimed, your son will live with peace of mind that the rightful owner received his or her property. This process will provide your son with the wherewithal to make future ethical choices.

What would you do?

Case 3

*You happen to come upon a car crash. You may
notice injured parties, or that no one seems hurt.
Many people "rubberneck" in order to satisfy their
curiosity. Typically, this traffic tie-up moves slowly
and when the scene of the accident is passed and
viewed by onlookers, the traffic moves at a
reasonable pace. However, the question remains,
"Should you stop at the accident scene, should you
tend to the parties involved, or should you summon
the police?" To compound the question, ask,
"Should you tend to the parties while waiting for
police or should you leave before the police arrive?"*

Whether there is injury or not, we are morally
obligated to contact emergency personnel. Tending
to an accident victim without sufficient medical
training could further debilitate the victim.
Although we may sympathize with the injured, we
cannot let our judgment be clouded. Often times,
operators at the 911 call center will ask you to
remain at the scene until help arrives. It is your
decision to make. Some may choose to leave the
scene since they fear being on the side of the road.
Others may leave since they believe they fulfilled
their obligation to summon help. Still others may

leave due to the fear of being in the presence of strangers. Finally, others leave the scene to avoid being called as a witness in court or to prevent medical malpractice litigation. Furthermore, safeguarding a scene by using your vehicle's emergency flashers or flairs, should you have them, to avoid additional collision or injury until rescue teams arrive, may be appropriate action. This author would safely stop and notify emergency personnel and await further instruction from the 911 operator.

What would you do?

Case 4

You are witness to a crime and are not sure if you should report it.

Police agencies rely on accurate witness accounts in the solving of crime and the swift apprehension of criminals. Naturally, it is not wise to place oneself in harm's way, so the dilemma lies with the fact that one must weigh the risks and benefits of reporting the crime. This author would make a mental note of the perpetrator's physical characteristics, his direction and mode of travel when fleeing the scene, and any noteworthy information. I would supply this information to the police since it is invaluable in an investigation. Failure to report to police could impede apprehension and lead to other innocent people becoming victims. It is difficult to make a rational decision based on proposed scenarios, yet in reality, all consequences have to be examined before making the choice to get involved. It is normal to assess the consequences of coming forth as a witness. If you choose to abstain coming forth, you could morally and emotionally suffer if you become aware that the perpetrator's actions affected other victims. Your moral fiber will assist you in making this decision.

What would you do?

Case 5

This dilemma has been heard before, but is worth repeating. You are asleep and your son comes home late at night, awakens you to tell you that he hit a person while driving and left the scene of the accident. He is unsure if the person is dead or alive; he only knows that the person was not moving while lying in the street. He does not believe that there were witnesses, but he cannot be certain of this. Obviously, he informs you of this in order to seek advice. Although the accident was not intentional, he was under the influence of alcohol. The failure to report the accident at the scene was a mistake on the part of your son, yet he comes to you for help in making a decision as to what to do and seeks your assurance that you will protect him. He has already made a decision, but unfortunately it was a wrong one. Having advised you of the event, you are now indirectly involved. You are faced with which decision should be instituted to correct the wrongdoings of your son.

There are many options including reporting the accident anonymously, leaving the situation as is, or the right choice of bringing your son back to the scene and calling a police officer. While it is difficult to surrender to a "hit and run" charge, the ethical choice is to have your son face up to the mistake and accept the consequences set forth by the law. As parents we must teach our children to make rational decisions which will enforce the values instilled in them. Regardless of the severity of the consequences that could be incurred, children learn by example. They follow the footsteps of those who rear them. Therefore it is important that we set the stage for the most ethically sound choices they can make. In order to enter society as a responsible adult, we first learn how to correct our mistakes and prevent others from happening. Sometimes we are dealt some compromising situations as parents who want only to protect our children, but we have to see clear to teach them to remain as morally straight as possible. If our children fall short of our expectations, we must learn to balance the disappointment with the moral obligation to lead them in the right direction. Standing behind them will prove that our love is unconditional and that we as parents will teach them how to deal with their indiscretions. In the end, if youth recognize the lessons learned from their parents or guardians, they will retain a complete moral character. They, in turn, take these lessons and pass them down to their children. They also realize that when life throws a curve ball, there is a way to rebound. The stronger the moral foundation, the stronger the ability will be to rebound and benefit from our mistakes.

What would you do?

Case 6

Your parents left strict instructions that you are not permitted to have guests in your house while they are not at home. Your friends who are aware that your parents are out show up unannounced and ready to party. Your guests are underage and have been consuming alcohol and possibly illegal substances. They continue to drink while in your home. One of your friends passes out and is unresponsive. Your other guests become scared and leave. You are faced with a decision to summon help or just let him "sleep it off."

Everything inside of you is telling you to get medical assistance for your friend. You know this will bring unwanted attention since you violated your parents' trust and the laws governing underage drinking. If you fail to act and your friend's condition deteriorates, or worse, he passes, you and your parents could be held legally and civilly responsible for the death. You will suffer lifelong feelings of enormous guilt.

What would you do?

Case 7

A friend confides in you regarding a recent diagnosis of a communicable disease, or thoughts of suicide, or confesses to being physically, sexually, or mentally abused, or has thoughts of harming others. What do you do with this information that you have been asked to hold in confidence?

I am a believer in upholding the confidence of a friend. If a friend wishes to confide in you and you cannot maintain this confidence, advise your friend of this. However, the aforementioned scenarios cannot be withheld and your friend should be made aware of this since they can adversely affect oneself or others. It must be explained that your friend needs to seek the assistance of family and trained professionals in order to protect oneself and others.

What would you do?

In conclusion, I suggest that everyone who reads this book define their values, place them on paper, and make them easily accessible at any time. Whenever you find yourself feeling challenged with a decision in your life, peruse your personal list of values and ask yourself, "Will this decision enhance or destroy who I am?" Our values define who we are and assist us in living a good life. We interpret society through our value system and in some instances lay down our lives for these beliefs. Additionally, ask yourself how your role models in life would view your actions and consider what they would do in a similar circumstance. Ask yourself, "What would your most admired person do in this situation?" It is taken for granted that we are programmed to know right from wrong, but in actuality when confusion exists, these simple steps of reviewing your values and mirroring your role models may be helpful in making the most appropriate decisions.

Chapter 9

Social Responsibility

"Are we aware of technology-- the social networking capabilities, its consequences, and its advantages? How can we be model citizens and how can we network to better ourselves and our communities?"

Modern technology has provided the world with many advantages. However, along with the upside comes the downside. Technology for purposes of this discussion will allude to computers, mobile devices to include cell phones, GPS systems, tablets, video and audio recorders, internet, and all handheld devices. The science of technology has allowed us to gain access to instant information and communication. It gives us the opportunity to speak to anyone in any part of the world at any time. It provides us with the information super highway which gives us answers to our questions as we demand. Technology is the inspiration for the future and gives us reason to invent, rebuild, and expand. Yet while all of this sounds positive, it cannot be ignored that there are negatives. For instance, it is possible for children to text their parents as to their whereabouts. In some cases, the whereabouts are not entirely known since there is no way to confirm the location of that text unless a device or application is implanted in the child's mobile phone. One main problem with use of these devices is that interpersonal skills are compromised since texting has replaced a great deal of oral communication. In addition, the proper syntax of the language has been severely modified. We have become complacent in arranging sentences to sound grammatically correct, and we have become comfortable in replacing words with slang terminology. The improper use of the language has spilled over in our formal writing. This could impact the impression we leave on others when we present our written information.

Through the internet we learn what is new and we remain current. We have information ranging from maps to facts at our fingertips. We have the ability to find our way when we get lost without unfolding a large paper map. Our cars are equipped with hands-free apparatus so we can carry on conversation while we drive. We use technology to multitask. We create infrastructure with computer graphic programs. We design clothes, toys, medicine, find our future spouses, earn degrees, and make music through the internet. News, weather, sports, and everything under the sun is reported through the internet. As a society, we have come to shy away from newspapers and have relied upon blogs (cyber news briefs and editorials). We began the process of genetic engineering, DNA testing and forensics, all with the aid of computers. It is amazing that a microscopic chip can store more information than one person could ever grasp in a lifetime. Still, so much information can become confusing and overwhelming, and it is often easy to misinterpret or misconstrue. We have lost the realization that it is humans who program the internet, and we have become subservient to some of the information it leads us to. It has caused some of us to take the information at face value rather than examining the facts. We have learned to accept the computer as the truth and have diminished the word delivered by mouth. Since there are so many facts and an infinite amount of internet avenues, we are prone to differences and mistakes as we attempt to draw conclusions.

Another realm of technology pertains to social networking websites. The advent of these sites opened up a whole new area of communication. As time passed the websites became more sophisticated and unleashed limitless possibilities to meet others from around the globe. The sites captivate users who sit at their computers and meet companions from the comfort of their desk chairs. The sites allow us to share recipes, likes, dislikes, and anything that could bond us as humans. It became easy to locate lost friends, reconnect with loved ones and learn of new lives and deaths on a minute-to-minute basis. Virtual tours from vacation spots, resorts, and private homes became popular. Trends and rumors begin on the websites and charitable causes profit from them. Advertising, false or otherwise, is flashed at us as quick as a blink of the eye. One dysfunction which seems to be escalating on social networking sites is cyber-bullying. This trend has unfortunately become more than occasional and has been a culprit in some tragic outcomes. One such event took place in 2010 when a young man attending college in New Jersey was the victim of his sexual orientation as it was paraded on a social network site after he was unknowingly photographed in a sexual act. This post was the predecessor to his tragic ending when he succumbed to his leap off a bridge. He saw no way out of the pain he felt from this heinous posting of his private life. This may not have caused his demise, but experts believed that there was a strong correlation between the cyber bullying and his inability to cope with the aftermath of it. Such acts are now considered crimes and are investigated when the bullying is volatile enough to show a relationship to inconceivable or irrational behavior. Experts advise that since September 11, 2001 there is no such thing as *anonymous.* No longer can one hide from his identity, even if he falsifies information. Security has been emphasized to preserve and protect the aggrieved. Through a warrant process anyone's social networking pages can be summoned. Information is easily validated through computer crime investigators. If it is proven that one has endangered or shown bias to another, the matter is taken into account and the individual responsible for this crime can be punished to the fullest extent of the law.

As human beings we possess many qualities that other living things do not; for instance, the ability to communicate with words, the creativity to better ourselves or society, and the techniques to compromise when it brings forth a meaningful solution. When we compromise these qualities we sometimes risk the redirection of our goals. This is harmful since goals drive us to succeed. Once we endanger our right to utilize our unique ways of communicating, we forfeit some of our basic principles. So if we depend on cell phones and email to bring forth messages (and they fail to be delivered) we must not assume that the receiver is not answering, but rather that the message was not received. A follow-up call is in order, yet we have relinquished landlines and rely on texting to push forward some vital information. Make no mistake about it, we must keep current with the technological trends but should not mistake technology for being infallible. After all, technology is only as good as those who devise it. Since humans design technology, it is subject to error. The amazing component of technology is that it enables us to communicate multiple messages and photographs to countless individuals to hundreds of locations in seconds! This brings us to another concern of technology; the channeling of information known as "sexting." Sexting, a dangerous and inappropriate act, uses mobile devices and computers to display provocative and sexually explicit messages through pictures and words. These messages which may start out as personal, are sent to select individuals and eventually proliferate in epidemic proportions. Shame, embarrassment and guilt are a few of the emotions connected to the person who is the unwilling participant of the spreading of these messages. Once sexually explicit material appears on the internet it can be easily deleted but just as easily retrieved and resurfaced at any time. In other words, "pictures are forever." I conferred with school social workers, psychologists, and guidance counselors who have advised me that a young individual would take part in a sexting act for three reasons. First, the person is attracted to the recipient of the message, secondly, the sender acts upon a "dare" from peers, and lastly, the sender lacks self-esteem. These reasons should not be perceived as justification for an act that could severely alter a person's life indefinitely in a negative way. Finally, your children may someday be able to access these messages on the internet.

Bullying comes in many forms including verbal, physical, exclusionary, and as previously mentioned, cyber. Verbal bullying takes form as the use of words, spoken or written, are used to disparage or intimidate; and is aggravated when sexual, racial, ethnic, and other biases are alluded to. Physical bullying includes assault, unwelcome physical contact and any act related to physical violence. Both verbal and physical bullying can include sexual harassment-- the unwelcome touching or spoken word with sexual overtones. *Exclusionary* bullying is defined when one or more persons are excluded from the mainstream and feel ostracized from the dominant group. This is an assault on one's personality and is destructive to self esteem. This happens in any age group, but is prevalent in adolescents and teens during the latter years of their public school education. Becoming sensitive to exclusion has become an uphill battle with the advent of social networking sites and electronic invitations. Since invitations are not sent through "snail mail" as first choice, others who are uninvited get wind easily of an event in which they are not selected to attend. This is hurtful and often done intentionally. In closing, the technology we embrace has afforded us quick and easy access to many avenues of society, yet has been the downfall in many of our values in the area of "*social responsibility.*"

In recent years, social host legislation has been enacted in many jurisdictions. This legislation is a milestone in social responsibility. The laws are particular to each state but serve to reinforce the same principles. Herein the primary resident, the adult eighteen years and older, is responsible for maintaining an orderly premise with respect to the consumption of alcoholic beverages. Through these laws, persons under legal drinking age (21 years of age) who are consuming alcohol under the watch of parents or other adults, become the reason for an arrest due to a host "knowingly" serving or providing alcohol. In cases where the adult claims that he or she is unaware of the alcohol being consumed in the home, law enforcement provides stipulations to define and sanction cases on an individual basis. For example, if a minor is injured due to alcohol consumption under the roof of the adult host, the primary focus is to protect the injured even though the drinking was illegal. The choice to drink may have solely been that of the minor, yet still a host is liable. A police officer may choose to enforce the stricter penal code in which fines and jail time are imposed with more stringent guidelines if the behavior is deemed as "endangering the welfare of a minor." While an offense of the social host laws brings forth a possible conviction of a misdemeanor, the possibility of injury due to driving while impaired brings forth a more rigid punishment, regardless of the drinker's age. The homeowners can be held criminally and/or civilly responsible for said offense since it occurred after drinking in their home.

It is the responsibility of the primary adult resident to take action should he or she become aware of illegal drinking. The correct course of action includes requesting the minor to cease drinking or reporting the incident. Should the minor refuse to cooperate, one can call local law enforcement authorities or a person who has more authority over the minor such as a parent or guardian. Insure that the one who consumed alcohol does not leave the premises unattended and awaits sobriety before departing as a driver or pedestrian. Escorting the person home by foot or cab is an example of responsible action by the host. It is recommended that parents check with their state or local police to ascertain a toll free number to anonymously report underage drinking. Calls of this nature may save lives. In addition, remain aware that the sale and distribution of alcohol to minors constitutes a serious offense which may be punishable by fines, imprisonment, or both. It is also imperative that when the use of illegal substances is suspected, that calls are placed to summon medical help if needed. Once again, it is ethically and socially responsible to summon emergency services regardless of the legal consequences. At times, teens fear to summon help because of the legal ramifications that may follow. Saving a life always precedes fear of disclosing illegal activity. Lastly, refer to local law enforcement agencies for the specifics of the social host laws in each state.

In conclusion, we all need to give back to the community in some way, shape, or form. There are many ways in which we can show civility. We can volunteer our time to the many organizations and institutions in society. We can donate money and skills to many who are in need. Good deeds such as shoveling a neighbor's driveway, picking up litter even though it is not ours, shopping for an elderly person, or just spending time conversing with someone in need of a friend are all tokens of civility and social responsibility. Finally, using sound judgment when using the internet and technology is paramount. The scale of these good deeds can be taken to levels above and beyond, but I live by the mottos of "what goes around comes around" and "no good deed goes unnoticed or unrewarded."

Appendix

"When you walked into this auditorium today you walked in with a platter full of education. This platter will become more plentiful as you further your education. I have just given you a side dish of life. What I would like you to do is go home, ingest what I gave you, digest what I gave you, and reflect. How do I want you to reflect? ...In a letter to me. Dear Paul, Dear Paulie, Dear Mr. Failla, Dear Officer Failla, and all I want you to tell me in that letter is what you as an individual got out of this program today. When you put pen to paper or fingers to keyboard you are simply amazing. I read every letter, and I save every letter. Future generations of my family will someday read your words." -- Paul D. Failla

The following pages contain messages of hope and inspiration and have touched Paul's heart. The words include comments regarding Paul's programs and were gathered from students, staff, teachers, parents, and administrators. The letters contributed bear no names for the purpose of preserving their sanctity. We respect the privacy of these participants as they shed light on the messages that Paul imparts and hope you are inspired by their words. Moreover, Paul gratefully recognizes their part in helping others to realize what strengths the workshops have given to the thousands who have attended. Paul wishes he could use all the testimonials received from the participants, but that would be a monumental task which would delay the publication of this book indefinitely. We invite you to view the "Written Testimonial" page of Paul's website at www.pdfailla.com for additional sentiments from various program participants.

Following are excerpts from over 4,000 letters Paul has received regarding his programs.

"I've had the pleasure of experiencing your presentations on teenage driving and prom responsibility. I say experience because it's impossible to simply just "attend." Your powerful

personality and engaging style are so different than what most folks expect, that one is immediately struck by your uniqueness—the ears perk up and the hands grip the seats as you weave story after story, lesson after lesson in a shocking, soulful style that reaches into the hearts and minds of your audience. No one leaves the same person as when he first walked in". ---Parent

*****

"When I heard we were going to have an assembly on Tolerance and Respect that would last two hours, I was a little reluctant. As soon as you began you hooked me in some kind of trance." ---High School Student

*****

"I really enjoyed the part of your program when you shared the stories about your father and the students you encountered over the years. It's really great to hear about ordinary students doing such extraordinary things. I hope that one day, I too, can do something that great and be considered a role model and possibly have you put my story in your "book." ---High School Student

"Some of the stories you told were so funny, yet others were so serious that I felt tears coming to my eyes. It is really incredible how big an impact you had on my emotions, and I'm hoping to live by your words for the rest of my life." --- High School Student

*****

"I can't remember the last time someone has captured my full attention like you did yesterday. You have impacted the way I think about myself, my family, my job, my beliefs and my priorities. I left wanting more. Thank you from the bottom of my heart. I will never forget what I learned about "me" that day."---Educational Administrator

*****

"I believe in everything you said. We need harmony. If I could stop wars I would." ---High School Student

*****

"Bullies are insecure. They bully to make themselves feel better."---High School Student

*****

"My mom is the greatest person to walk this earth in my eyes (same for my sister and proud father). I let

her know this every night. I love you mom."---High School Student

*****

"Mr. Paul Failla's presentation resonated acutely with me. Through his heartfelt rendering of other people's devastating misfortunes, I was able to highlight all the wonderful things to be grateful for."---Parent

*****

"Your presentation impacted my life greatly. I will never make fun of anyone again, I promise to show compassion to everyone and I will accept others for who they genuinely are. I am a better person because of you. I could never show just how thankful I am to have had you make me see what really matters."---Middle School Student

*****

"The thing that really stood out in my mind was when you told us the story about the man who called himself "Robin Hood," and how you brought him into the police station where he was verbally abused. I think the way that you stood up to the other police officer shows how compassionate and

humane you are, and I give my utmost respect and admiration."   ---Middle School Student

*****

"Speechless, tearful, proud, astonished. I have experienced all of these emotions, and more today. With every breath you took, every uttered word, I found myself locked into everything you said." --- High School Student

*****

"You have touched me today like no one else so far was ever able to do. I love you for that."   ---High School Student

*****

"Well I was thinking about what you said about the whole bully thing and I'm not a bully but I did bully people around, you know how it is. Afterwards I went up to that person and said that I was sorry. I mean I know how it feels. Look at me, I mean seriously I have five inch spikes and I wear ripped pants and what not. How am I not a perfect target for someone to make fun of? But I don't care. It doesn't bother me one bit. I am who I want to be and no one will stop me from being that. I thank u

for coming to our school and sharing all your
thoughts and everything you have been through."---
High School Student

*****

"You never know how something that one individual
says or does can change the destiny of others. The
value of what Paul does through his messages just
may detour someone's path enough to save a life."--
-Parent

*****

"Loyalty, allegiance, equality, justice, and making
the right choices in life are some of the themes that
stood out in your speeches. All of these qualities
that you discussed are those that I will try my best to
have in my life. Thank you."---College Student

*****

"The assembly gave me chills, made me cry, and
laugh hysterically. It made me look deep down in
my heart. I did, and I apologized to anyone I've ever
bullied. I put myself in their shoes for thirty seconds
and couldn't take it anymore. I witnessed some
teasing that day which could have led to something
worse, and for the first time I pulled that person

aside and told them to walk a mile in the other person's shoes."---Middle School Student

*****

"You're very knowledgeable of what the world is, and it is a monster, but it's up to us as individuals to make it that way or not make it that way. I like how you remind people to remember who they are and where they come from. "---College Student

*****

"After he died, so did Christmas. Happiness has been replaced with despair. Depression has overcome joy... Jamie, my brother, touched so many lives and made a difference in so many ways, just as you have, Officer, and I thank you. You are making a difference. God Bless and may you stay forever young."---High School Student

*****

"Just remember every time you hold my hand you still get to touch dad because I am made from him. It's kind of like holding dad's hand.....This quote is from my son after the death of my husband. I am so honored to have my son's story in your book, as was Bryan. To have Bryan included in your book with the

likes of Brooke Ellison, Stephon Marbury, and of course, your dad, truly touches my heart."---Parent/Educator

*****

"The program made me realize how bad my relationship was with my parents. When Mr. Failla was done talking, I told him how I felt and he helped me. He called my mom up to school and helped to start a new chapter of my life. The next day, I fixed things with my dad. Now I'm much happier and so are my parents all thanks to Mr. Failla."---Middle School Student

*****

"The decisions you make not only reflect you, but also the people around you. Loyalty and values are the most important assets to being a decent human being. The decisions I make for the rest of my life will always be based on my values and the values my parents instilled in me since I was a little boy."---College Student

*****

'Today is here but tomorrow is not guaranteed.'
"You made me realize that life is too short not to

acknowledge the people who matter most in your life. And you taught me that my actions won't only affect me but also the people around me." --- High School Student

*****

"I've never had a relationship with my dad but after hearing you speak about your father it made me want to reconnect with him."---High School Student

*****

"What I learned today will never escape my mind. I learned that life may be short and that every second counts. So today, I'm going to say, "I love you" to my parents. I agree that teasing is wrong, racism and discrimination are wrong, and that family and friends appear to be the best people you can ever ask for." ---High School Student

*****

"You've made me think about my life in the way that everyone should. It's such a precious thing and it should never be taken for granted. I knew that was true but never gave it much thought or put it to practice. You helped me to appreciate the smallest things in my life because I never know when it's all

going to be taken away from me. Thank you for everything you said because it truly changed my life."---College Student

*****

"Every time you have left this classroom I've felt refreshed and ready to live my life better than I have yesterday. You made me think about how I have treated people in the past and how I want to treat them in the future. I will live my life through love, honesty and the faith that everything happens for a reason. I cannot thank you enough." ---College Student

*****

"You showed me how to believe in myself and others. You also showed me to never give up on my dreams."---Elementary School Student

*****

"No one was afraid to admit that they were teary-eyed today or fearful of being ridiculed by classmates for 'feeling' today, for showing their emotions. I really think that was a wonderful gift you gave us. I'm the kind of person who has empathy for everyone; occasionally my sympathy for

people is a bit ridiculous. I've begun to lose any empathy for relatives of mine. I wish they all could have heard from you when they were freshman in high school. I think they wouldn't be as self-centered. I could have had one of those families with unconditional love for each other. From the moment you said we could write letters, I knew I had to. But once I came to that conclusion I asked myself why would he care about a letter from just another person; a person whose face was lost among the sea of hundreds of faces he saw today? I think that's why I wanted to write because I sensed that you would read all the letters. Generally, I am not impressed or inspired by people, but what you have done today was so indescribable. Just as the decisions we make affect so many people, what you have taught all of us today will affect many more."-- -Middle School Student

*****

"It is a rare gift to encounter a person who can continue to motivate others to redirect and revisit their lives. It is without question that I have been touched and am more dedicated to my profession since I first saw Paul Failla speak nine years ago. I have extracted much information from his various

topics which helps me implement life lessons in my classes. In addition, the programs have prompted me to redefine my values and have given me more incentive to remain passionate about my profession."---College Professor

*****

"Your messages of common sense, courtesy, abstinence, truth, and discipline, along with the advice on how to withstand peer pressure has a powerful positive impact on your audiences. You actively save lives with these presentations."---Parent

*****

"The truth is, when Paul speaks he saves lives. Paul teaches respect, commitment, integrity, and good judgment.... Clinging to every word, seventeen and eighteen year-old young men and women embraced his message, laughed at all his jokes and were inspired by his stories. When they attend the prom, move on to college, and step into the real world, these students will think about the consequences before they get behind the wheel."---High School Social Studies Teacher

"Paul has the ability to reach all ages, all attitudes, personalities, and ethnic origins with his message. He is able to disarm the most cynical in the audience. ---Representative, Boy Scouts of America

Acknowledgements

From Paul and Nancy

We thank the many people which include family, friends, personal and professional acquaintances, living and deceased, who have contributed to the success of this project. Without their dedication to the writer and editor, this book would not have been possible. For their significant acts of kindness and unselfish character, we are grateful and proud to have them in our lives. Their willingness to perpetuate humanity in its finest will live on in these messages.

Editor's Note

*I met Paul Failla in 2003 at an area high school when I attended his "Character Education" program. At the time, I was involved with another parent in a drug education curriculum offered by the county police department in which Paul served. We attended countless workshops on risky behavior and thought that Paul's would be the typical power point presentation that we had become so familiar with. As an educator in the Social Sciences, I had prepared so many seminars in drug prevention and disease, and was saturated with information on various behaviors. To my surprise, I had received a wealth of information through Paul's workshop. At the conclusion of the program, I introduced myself to Paul (I waited on a line with many other parents who wanted to express their thanks to Paul for an eventful evening) and we exchanged email addresses. Shortly thereafter, I invited Paul to speak to my college classes. He has addressed my classes since then. In 2007, Paul approached me with the job of editing his website, which was successfully launched a few months after its inception. I was honored to have taken part in this project, particularly since it was sponsored by a grateful parent who attended Paul's Driver Safety Awareness Program with his son. That was a debt of gratitude that I was proud to be a part of. As I take on outside projects, I am selective. Paul's book, **Life: 101** is certainly a project worth editing. It provides the* *readers with a taste of his various programs and combines humor, drama, and common sense to relay life's most important moral messages.*

Nancy G. DiMonte, Editor

Paul D. Failla

Paul D. Failla, born in Queens, New York is a retired twenty-seven year veteran of the Suffolk County Police Department on Long Island. Paul graduated from Plainedge High School, North Massapequa, New York and received an Associate Degree in Business from Farmingdale State College, New York. He devised a series of motivational programs for students ranging from fifth grade through college during his time as a Suffolk County police recruitment officer and has become a sought after educational consultant nationwide. Paul travels to relay messages of vital importance to the youth of America. His assemblies focus on character education, diversity issues, bullying, risky behaviors, and driver safety awareness. Paul's messages are riveting as they are executed in unconventional, yet inspirational ways. Students have come to embrace his style of teaching. In addition to student programs, Paul offers workshops to parents, educators, administration, and staff throughout schools from New York to California, to include training in Ethical Awareness. He has been a keynote speaker in several educational conventions as well as graduation ceremonies throughout area high schools. Mr. Failla has presented at the New York State Bar Association's Law, Youth and Citizenship Statewide Conferences, New York State Social Studies and Supervisory Association Conventions, the Long Island Council for the Social

Studies, the New York State Association of Police Chiefs Conference, and the New York State Division of Criminal Justice Services Bureau for Municipal Police. These are among the many highlights of his speaking engagements. In addition, Paul is a professional actor and has had roles in film, regional theater and has performed Off-Broadway. He is a member of the Screen Actors Guild and has accumulated numerous awards for his educational repertoire. Paul is a recipient of the 2011 Nassau County, New York BOCES "Education Partner Award." Paul has two daughters, Gioia and Maria, a son-in-law, Jay, and resides in New York with his wife, Dale, and Bella, their pet Schnauzer.

Nancy G. DiMonte

Nancy G. DiMonte, born in Manhattan, New York received a Bachelor of Arts Degree in Health Education with a focus in Social and Behavioral Sciences from the City University of New York at Queens College. She received a Master of Arts Degree in Liberal Studies with a concentration in Social and Behavioral Sciences from the State University of New York at Stony Brook. Nancy currently teaches Sociology in the New York State University system. She has published articles in various local newspapers and is an advocate of substance abuse/ prevention education. Nancy coauthored a textbook geared towards success for college freshmen and has taught an array of courses related to behavioral sciences. She conducts a myriad of self–help workshops to include topics such as suicide, domestic violence, and disease prevention. In addition to her support of many community service organizations, Nancy edits college admission essays for high school seniors and reviews upcoming college textbooks. Nancy has two children Joelle and Joey, and lives on Long Island.

Notes

Paul D. Failla

Notes

Notes

Life:101

25894911R00108

Made in the USA
Charleston, SC
18 January 2014